WOVEN

Tabara
N'Diaye

Make Your Own
Accessories from
Raffia, Rope and Cane

WOVEN

Tabara
N'Diaye

quadrille

To the present and future generations
of makers, may these pages be an
inspiration, weaving hands, hearts
and souls together.

To Senna, whose light enlightens each
and every one of my creative projects.

Contents

Introduction

Living in London, one of the fashion capitals of the world, offers a front-row seat to witness trends explode onto the scene. And from the bustling streets of Soho to the prestigious catwalks of London Fashion Week, there is one trend that has caught my attention: woven accessories featuring prominently in everyday life and style.

Traditionally perceived as a summertime staple – think a basket bag, straw hat or espadrilles – woven accessories have evolved to showcase their adaptability for all seasons. Fashion designers have ingeniously incorporated woven elements into autumn and winter collections, presenting cosy knits and outerwear adorned with woven accents. Basket bags are lined with warm fabrics and basket-weaving techniques are applied to a wide range of materials to create everything from footwear to headwear.

Of course, I may be a little bit biased. My love for all things baskets has its roots in my Senegalese heritage, a country well known for its colourful coiled baskets brightening up local markets, and it was also the inspiration behind my first book, *Baskets*. But really, this newfound appreciation for basket-weaving makes total sense, as craftsmanship and sustainability are two trends resonating with a generation that values authenticity and mindful consumption.

While my previous book focused on weaving baskets and accessories for your living space, this follow-up has come as the perfect little sister to *Baskets* to give you the tools and inspiration to weave fashionable accessories into your everyday style. I've made sure to include projects that are more approachable, with materials that are easier to find (and stylish alternatives) while still using techniques to be preserved and celebrated.

With a more fashion-led book, it feels really important to touch on some of the challenges the fashion industry has been facing. And to reflect on how we, as crafters, can continue to be active participants in the movement towards sustainability by repurposing and upcycling, thus contributing to a more conscious, caring and WOVEN world.

A lot has changed since I first sat down at my keyboard in 2017, and I've loved watching more and more people embrace crafting and basket-weaving since then. Of course, as a creative outlet, but also as a way to give new life to what was already at home when we couldn't go anywhere and, most importantly, to provide a sense of comfort and therapeutic relief to help combat the feelings of isolation and anxiety that many experienced in 2020.

My mission, if you still accept it, remains the same: to continue to shine light on basket-weaving with modern, playful and accessible projects. Weaving together the threads of tradition and creativity, basketry and style are truly intertwined.

The evolution of basket-weaving in fashion

In the modern fashion world, the revival of age-old craft techniques has emerged as a significant trend and in recent years basket-weaving has become a key player. A practice with origins that can be traced back to ancient civilizations – the oldest woven basket in the world was found in the Middle East in 2021 and dates back 10,000 years – has been resurrected in contemporary design with a newfound sense of creativity and innovation. Designers keen to incorporate unique textures and sustainable materials into their collections have found inspiration in the multiple techniques used to weave baskets. What was once viewed as a utilitarian craft, to create containers for gathering food, water and other necessities, has now evolved into a skill that complements haute couture on runways and trickles down to everyday wear.

Sustainable fashion

At the core of this basket-weaving revolution lies the global movement towards sustainable fashion. As climate change and environmental concerns become urgent global issues, the fashion industry is facing more scrutiny for its impact on the planet on a daily basis. Fast fashion's unsustainable practices are leading consumers to seek alternatives that promote ethical production and mindful consumption. And basketry, with its emphasis on natural materials and handcrafted techniques, offers just that. By weaving with natural fibres, such as grasses, bamboo and leaves, to name a few, designers embrace the planet in all its beauty and encourage a more responsible approach to fashion.

From France with love

In France, where I grew up, basket bags are a wardrobe staple and it's always fascinated me to see how synonymous they are with French style around the world – casual yet sophisticated.

It was in the 1970s that the basket bag was brought into the limelight thanks to Jane Birkin, an English actress and singer, partner of French national treasure Serge Gainsbourg. Birkin was often photographed carrying a straw basket bag, making it the final touch to her signature style of a simple white shirt and flared jeans. Decades later, her images still adorn many Pinterest style boards and her name is often referenced as the one who started the basket bag revolution.

To the catwalks of the world

In today's fashion landscape, woven elements are taking centre stage on the catwalks of many fashion weeks around the world, as designers incorporating basket-weaving techniques into their collections have elevated a traditionally humble item to a luxury product.

Dolce & Gabbana led the way with a Spring/Summer 2013 collection featuring rattan bustiers and corsets adorned with black tulle. Since then, numerous leading fashion houses have followed suit, such as Christian Dior, with its Spring/Summer 2019 collection showcasing long pastel dresses reminiscent of the twill-weaving technique, and Oscar de la Renta, with its Pre-Fall 2023 collection that included a raffia cupcake cocktail dress.

Recent collaborations between esteemed designers, such as Loewe, Chanel and Chloé, and skilled artisan weavers, have further bridged the gap between traditional craftsmanship and contemporary fashion.

But it's not just the high-end market that has had its eye on this trend. With woven details adorning oversized jackets, hoodies and even footwear infusing a touch of bohemian elegance to the everyday person's style, this trend is showing no sign of slowing down.

Basket-weaving and mindfulness

One of the most profound impacts of basket-weaving's integration into fashion has been its role in encouraging mindfulness and a return to slow crafting. In an era dominated by digital distractions and the relentless pursuit of instant gratification, basket-weaving is a gentle reminder of slow creation, where an accessory can sometimes take days or weeks to be finished. This mindfulness aspect resonating with fashion designers and consumers alike is continuing to encourage a shift towards quality over quantity and cherishing the stories behind what we wear.

Today, the evolution of baskets from humble household items to coveted fashion pieces stands as a testament to the legacy of this traditional craft and its ability to find a place of prominence in both fashion and interior design.

Why make?

I still cherish the memory of weaving my first drink coaster. Despite its slight imperfections – being a tad wonky and not perfectly flat – it remains a treasured memento. It might not be the ideal surface on which to place a drink, but the sense of accomplishment and pride it instils in me pretty much sums up why making is invaluable.

When I began my journey with basket-weaving, my professional career as a busy events manager travelling around the country was my number-one priority. What really drew me in was the mindfulness and tranquillity I instantly felt, rather than the end result alone. Had I fixated solely on the finished pieces, I might have abandoned my new hobby a long time ago.

Making became my haven from the outside noise. I found solace in the rhythmic and repetitive steps, often losing track of time and my to-do list, immersing myself fully in the craft. This, to me, is the true beauty of making, and its superpower.

Much in the same way as some people embrace baking or journalling, crafting became my mindful practice and essential to my day-to-day routine. But don't just take my word for it – numerous studies have been published discussing the positive impact of making on personal growth, mental wellbeing, anxiety management and stress relief.

This won't come as a surprise to you, but we live in a world where personal style is often dictated by fast fashion and fleeting trends. Crafting is the perfect antidote and the perfect way to express yourself. Making encourages you to tap into your creativity, play around with colours, textures and patterns while continuing to foster a sense of individuality and authenticity.

Crafting also allows you to build a deeper and personal connection to your creations. I often say that once you've made your first basket in a couple of hours, you will have a deeper appreciation for the faithful woven laundry basket that you have in the corner of your bedroom, with its very intricate pattern that took days, sometimes weeks, to be completed.

And of course, I couldn't discuss the benefits of making without touching on the sustainable side of things. It undoubtedly encourages us to be more mindful consumers, valuing quality over quantity, therefore leading to a more sustainable way of living.

PANTONE 19-2025
Red Plum

PANTONE 18-0119
Willow Bough

PANTONE 18-1248
Rust

PANTONE
152

TABARA

Finding inspiration

In the hustle and bustle of modern life, when we are constantly bombarded with information and our senses are continuously engaged, taking a moment to seek inspiration is not just a luxury but also a necessity.

For me, inspiration is intertwined with my creativity, providing a fresh lens through which I view my craft, and I find it in various places and experiences.

Having grown up in Paris, where people-watching could almost be considered a national sport, I developed a habit of studying passersby while sipping a café noisette at my local bistro. I found joy in admiring, and being inspired by, people's unique styles and absorbing the diverse energies they brought to the urban landscape. In London, my current home, the pace may be different but the streets still offer a melting pot that fuels my creativity.

As for many others, travelling has been a source of inspiration for me over the years. From the bustling markets of Dakar, which inspired me to start La Basketry, to the vibrant streets of Havana, I always come back from a trip not only with a suitcase filled with baskets, but also inspired by new cultures, landscapes and ways of living.

Closer to home, if you have access to them, local museums and exhibitions are great places to get a more regular dose of inspiration. Standing in front of a piece of art, I often find myself transported to a different era and perspective, sparking new connections and conversations. That, to me, is the real beauty of visual arts and how they ignite my own desire to create.

Being an avid enthusiast for all crafts, I am always fascinated by other disciplines and wondering how materials or tools from a punch needle class or pottery, for instance, could enrich my own work. Using my hands in a different way and then coming back to my own craft always gives me a fresh perspective and a wealth of new ideas.

In the digital age, online platforms such as Pinterest have become a virtual treasure trove of inspiration that cannot be overlooked. It is a world where images, ideas and quotes all meet and serve as a reminder that imagination has no boundaries.

A few years ago, I stumbled upon this quote from the Ghanaian author Lailah Gifty Akita: 'In the midst of our daily lives, we must find the magic that makes our souls soar.' To me, this beautifully embodies what inspiration should be and is a daily reminder to be present and attentive to the world around us and to find sources of inspiration in the small joys, challenges and experiences of our everyday lives.

How to use this book

Whether you're a seasoned crafter or a complete novice, I've devised this book as the perfect companion for exploring basket-weaving and guiding you in translating your unique style into beautiful and stylish woven pieces for everyday life.

Demystifying basketry, which is often perceived as either too complex or outdated, lies at the heart of *Woven*. I want to assure you that embarking on this journey doesn't require a quest for rare materials (unless you'd like to) as most supplies can be found at your local haberdashery shop, and I strongly encourage you to breathe new life into old fabrics and materials as you find your groove.

Like many other crafts, basket-weaving has many techniques that have travelled and migrated across the world with populations, evolving over time as they merge with different cultures. I've chosen to focus on three techniques that have always resonated with me and suit my lifestyle as a mother living in a big city with minimal storage.

Drawing inspiration from my Senegalese roots and the vibrant baskets that captured my heart during my childhood, the opening chapter focuses on the 'Coiling' technique, guiding you through the process of wrapping and stitching strands of raffia into jewellery and accessories.

In the next chapter, 'Cane', I shift my focus to the 'stake and strand' technique, working with centre cane, softening the material by soaking it in water and then bending it and shaping it during the weaving process.

The final chapter, 'Braiding', delves into the world of plaiting, using three, four or five strands, to create everything from a simple headband to a stylish backpack. It's an open invitation to experiment with different patterns to add a personal touch to your creations.

Before diving into each chapter's projects, you'll find an introductory 'how to', which will help you to familiarize yourself with key steps, materials and terminology. I've also sprinkled in some styling tips and delved into some key trends as we move towards a more sustainable and environmentally conscious approach to crafting.

The measurements and quantities given serve as guidelines, but the dexterity of your hands, the tightness of your weave and the quality of the materials you use will all play a huge part in the finished result as you start making.

Finally, as I often like to emphasise in my workshops, basket-weaving requires patience, practice and a willingness to learn. And if you've picked up this book, it suggests you might just be the perfect candidate.

Materials

Crafting begins with the very foundations of your projects: the materials. Much more than purely practical 'ingredients', they are the heartbeat, the soul and the core of your makes. The importance of sourcing high-quality materials cannot be overstated as they set the tone for your entire creative process and contribute significantly to the outcome of your projects.

Here are the three main materials used for the projects in this book:

Raffia

Derived from the leaves of the Raffia palm (*Raphia farinifera*), which is native to Madagascar and other parts of Africa, raffia boasts a rich history deeply intertwined with traditional crafting practices. Known for its versatility, it has become a staple material that is easily accessible in craft and haberdashery shops all around the world. Its popularity comes from the ease with which it can be incorporated into everything from basketry and flower arrangements to macramé and gift wrapping. Typically sold in bundles or hanks and measured by length or weight, raffia takes to dyeing very easily, allowing you to create a rainbow of colours for your makes.

Cotton rope

This material needs no introduction. Widely used across a range of crafts, cotton rope has its origins in the natural fibres of the cotton plant, making it a sustainable choice for your projects.

Cotton rope often comes braided, where individual cotton fibres are intricately woven or twisted together, piped in a tubular shape, twisted or twined.

A diameter of 6–8mm (¼–⁵⁄₁₆ inch) is preferred for the projects in this book. Purchasing it in rolls of 50m (54.7 yards) or 75m (82 yards) proves to be the most cost-effective way to work with it.

Centre cane

Derived from the Rattan palm (*Calamus rotang*), centre cane or rattan is a familiar material in the world of basketry. Harvested from the inner layers of the palm native to Southeast Asia, it can be used for furniture, home decor or even outdoor products such as garden fencing.

In its natural state, centre cane is too brittle to be woven so it requires pre-soaking in lukewarm water, transforming it into a pliable and workable material.

Storing centre cane properly is crucial to maintaining its quality. Ideally, it should be kept in a cool, dry place away from direct sunlight to prevent it from drying out or becoming overly brittle.

It is usually sold in reels measured by weight and available in a variety of sizes (please see the size chart on page 22 for guidance on the sizes used in this book).

Centre cane conversion chart

This handy conversion chart is intended to help basket-makers who are not working in metric measurements with the projects in this book.

If you are unable to find the exact thickness required for the projects, don't hesitate to round up to the next size.

UK number	No. 3	No. 5	No. 6	No. 8	No. 10	No. 14
Diameter (mm)	2.00	2.5	2.65	3.00	3.3	4.25
US number	No. 2.5	No. 3	No. 4	No. 4.5	No. 5	No. 6.5
Diameter (inches)	$5/64$	$3/32$	$7/64$	$1/8$	$9/64$	$3/16$

Tools

Whether you're a seasoned basket-maker or just starting your journey, having the right tools is crucial. Here's a comprehensive list of tools to help you create beautiful accessories and baskets.

Basket-maker's bodkin or sewing awl
An essential tool for working with cane and other materials, a basket-maker's bodkin is ideal for piercing through cane when creating a base and making gaps for weaving. A good alternative is a sewing awl, often used for heavy materials including leather.

Cane cutters
Required for cutting centre cane, these cutters are versatile and handy for various materials.

Masking tape
Ideal for securing purposes, especially when working with raffia and braiding.

Measuring tape
Essential for measuring lengths of cane, rope and raffia, and to help you keep an eye on the size and height of your projects as you go along.

Needles
Different types of needles are required. Long-eyed needles are perfect for the coiling projects, whereas curved needles are very handy for the plaiting ones, for sewing and shaping braids of raffia into accessories.

Extra-strong thread
A must-have when you need to do a little bit of hand sewing.

Pegs and clips
Essential for holding materials in place so things don't unravel. They can also provide stability during the weaving process.

Scissors
Sharp scissors are necessary for cutting materials and thread with precision.

Pins
Handy for temporarily securing elements in place while working on intricate patterns.

Rubber bands and string
Useful for bundling materials together and securing them during various stages of basket-making.

Basket bases
These pre-drilled wooden bases crafted specifically for basketry come in various sizes and shapes (oval, rectangular, circular, square).

Extra bits

Sewing machine and fabric
For projects involving fabric elements –
for example, creating lining for some of the
basket bags.

Bucket
Handy for soaking and preparing materials,
such as cane, before weaving.

Pliers
Useful for gripping, bending and manipulating
centre cane as you start to build up your projects.

Utility knife
Handy for trimming and shaping materials, as
well as cutting cardboard pieces to make moulds.
Make sure you always use it carefully.

Weights
Helpful for keeping certain elements in place
as the weaving progresses. I use bricks from the
garden to hold my braiding in place.

Leather straps
These can be used to add a decorative and
functional element to your accessories, such
as handles and straps for basket bags.

Spray varnish
This gives your finished item a protective finish
and enhances its visual appeal.

Frameless mirror pieces
Often used in mosaic art and DIY home decor,
frameless mirror pieces are a versatile crafting
element that work brilliantly in basket-weaving.

Wood glue
Used with the basket bases to ensure a strong
foundation for your project.

Hand towel
Keep one nearby when working with centre
cane, especially since you'll be repeatedly

dipping your hands into the bucket of water
to pick up soaked bundles of cane.

Buttons
The perfect finishing touch to accessories
such as basket bags.

Fabric
Use fabric to create a lining for some of
your projects.

Beads
Perfect to add texture, colour and playfulness
to personalize your makes.

Earring hooks
Used to attach jewellery to the earlobe, making
them wearable.

Headband blank
Serves as the foundation for making woven
headbands, perfect to personalize with a variety
of weaving techniques and materials.

Pinking shears
Used to cut fabric or ribbon with a zigzag edge,
preventing fraying and adding a playful finish to
your makes.

Round cake dummy
Provides a stable base for shaping and forming
round accessories, ensuring uniformity in size
and shape.

Velvet ribbon
Adds the final decorative touch to some of your
projects. Play around with textures and finishes.

Spray water bottle
Helps to dampen cane when you don't
necessarily want to soak it, making it easier to
manipulate during the weaving process.

Additional tools that are useful to have
Ruler, pencil, adhesive tape, cardboard,
fabric glue, and microfibre cloth.

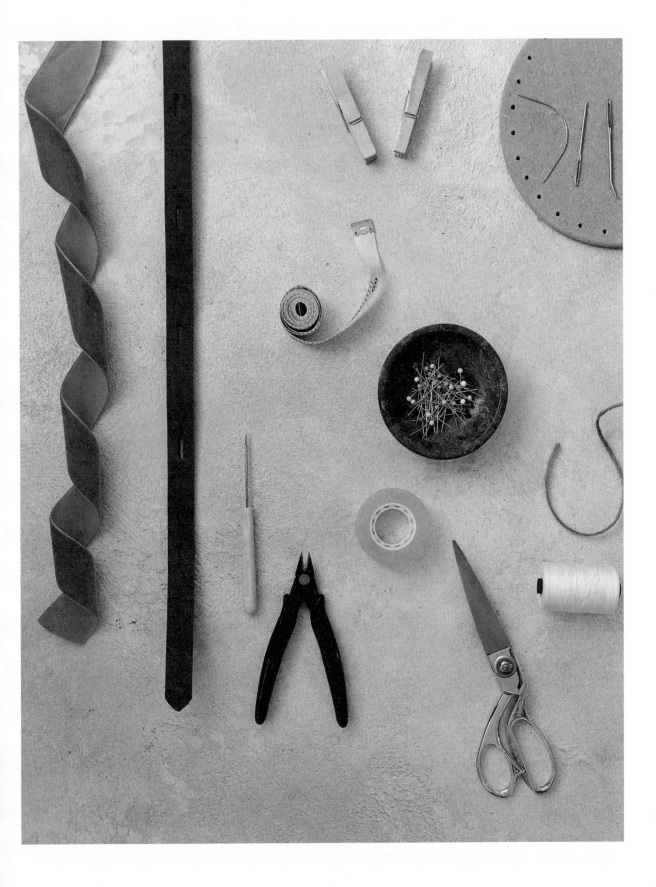

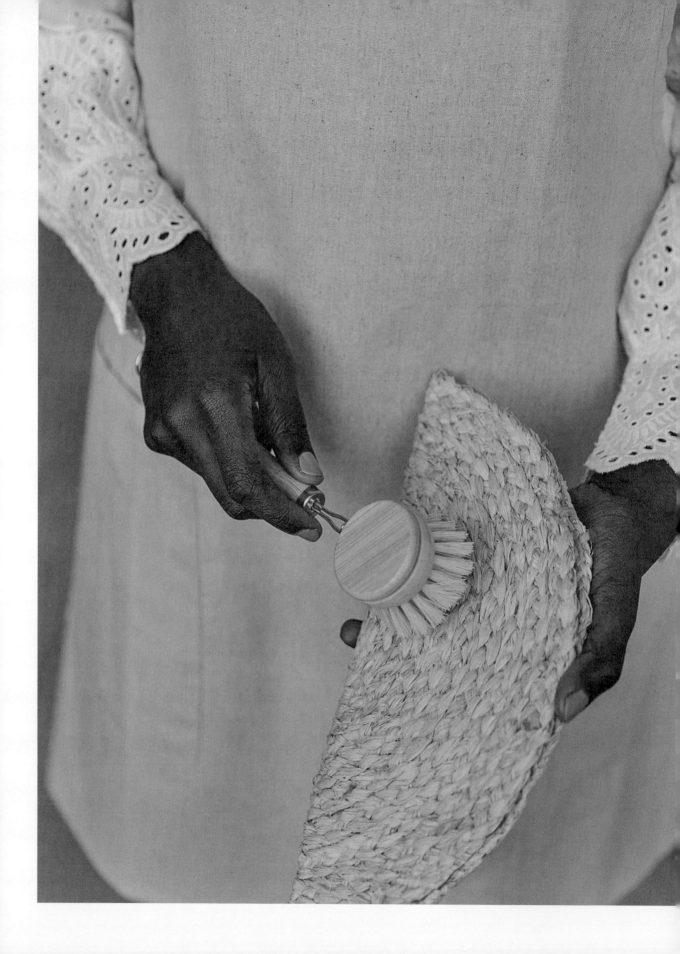

How to care for your pieces

Just like any other items in your wardrobe that you love and treasure, your woven accessories deserve some special care to ensure they stand the test of time.

1. Say no to moisture

Given that your accessories are woven with natural fibres, it's best to avoid wearing them in the rain and stay away from damp environments. I know this is easier said than done if, like me, you live in a country such as the UK where it rains for, on average, 150 days a year. If one of your pieces does get wet, allow it to air-dry naturally – while it may be tempting to use a hairdryer to speed up the process, don't, as it can lead to the materials becoming brittle.

2. Cleaning

Dust can easily settle in the weaving or gaps, so stay on top of it by regularly using a soft brush or cloth; a clean toothbrush can also do the trick on small items. Accidents and spillages do happen. In such cases, you can use a damp soft cloth, cold water and a mild detergent, but be cautious of excessive moisture and make sure you don't over-saturate the raffia or centre cane. If all else fails, you can always consider dyeing the accessory a darker shade; for tips on this, please refer to the natural dyeing section (see pages 51).

Over time, you may notice some flyaway fibres, from the braiding, for example. If that's the case, just trim them off with a pair of sharp scissors.

3. Travelling and packing tips

Whenever I'm travelling and need to pack some of my woven accessories, I always place my hats flat at the bottom of my suitcase with their crowns lightly stuffed with soft items such as scarves. I also stuff my basket bags and make sure to place them in the centre of the suitcase, away from the edges. My preference is to use a case with a hard shell or rigid frame.

4. Reshaping with steam

If you notice that one of your raffia bags or accessories has become misshapen in transit, or in your wardrobe, you can use steam to fix it. Hold the bag over a pot of boiling water or set your iron to the 'steam' setting. The steam will gently soften the raffia and you can then reshape it.

5. Storage

When they are not in use, store your woven pieces in a cool, dry place away from direct sunlight. To maintain their shape, I like to stuff my hats and basket bags with tissue paper or old newspaper and place them in fabric drawstring bags to protect them from dust.

Coiling

Coiling

My love affair with baskets and basket-weaving blossomed on the vibrant streets of Thies, my parents' hometown in Senegal. Amidst the hustle and bustle of daily life, I was always captivated by the intricate spiral patterns, diverse shapes, and vibrant colours of coiled baskets lining the busy roads and available to purchase at local markets.

Coiling, often described as 'a sewing technique that consists of sewing a spiral foundation securely in a coil and wrapping this coil with another material threaded through a needle and sewn over the coils', may seem daunting at first glance. Yet, mastering this technique is surprisingly achievable with a bit of practice (see pages 32–35 for detailed instructions).

The journey of coiling techniques spans continents, carried by the winds of migration. From the tightly wound vessels of Native American tribes to down under, where Aboriginal communities weave coiled baskets from local grasses and fibres. Observing similar techniques adapted by diverse cultures around the globe is endlessly fascinating.

For this section, I've chosen raffia as the main core material – it's easily accessible, cost-effective, and a popular choice for coiling. However, grasses, straw, rope, cordage, and sometimes wire can be used, while not forgetting materials you may already have at home that can be repurposed for a project (see page 45 for some tips).

How-to

This section will walk you through the fundamental steps of weaving a coiled basket using raffia. Learn how to start your base, add in new core and stitching material, shape and complete your basket.

For more guidance mastering this basketry technique, watch a comprehensive video tutorial featuring essential steps, along with helpful tips at www.labasketry.com/pages/woven.

Before you begin, gather your materials.

Materials
5–7 strands of raffia in a bundle (the core)
1 piece of raffia for stitching (the stitching material)
Long-eyed needle
1 peg
1 pair of scissors

1. Starting the base

Hold the core bundle with your left hand and, with your right hand, start wrapping the stitching material around the ends of the core, leaving a gap of 1cm (⅜ inch) at the tip, and making 5 clockwise wraps (towards you) around the core. If you are left-handed, you might find it easier to hold the bundle with your right hand and wrap with your left.

Fold the just-wrapped core into two to create a little eyelet. Wrap the stitching material around the base of the eyelet to secure it, then use your peg to hold it in place and prevent it from unravelling.

Thread your needle onto the other end of the stitching material, and tie a little knot to prevent it from slipping off as you start weaving. Then, poke it through the central hole of the eyelet.

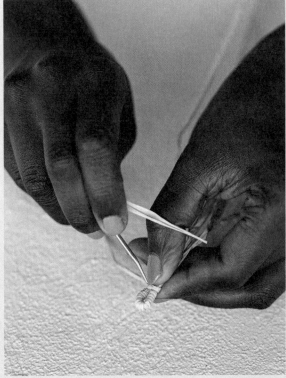

2. Coiling the basket

Start to coil the core into a circle. Follow this pattern: wrap the stitching material clockwise around the bundle for approximately 1cm (⅜ inch), or 4–5 wraps, and stitch by inserting your needle through the central hole of the eyelet. Repeat this step until you complete a full round.

Continue with the same pattern of wrapping and stitching, ensuring the stitches overlap the current and previous rounds of your coil (one row below).

3. Joining new materials

To join in new core material, take another 5–7 strands of raffia and wrap them around the rest of the bundle. Secure with a peg, then continue wrapping and stitching as before with your stitching material.

To join in new stitching material (or change colour), lay the new strand of raffia at the front of your coil, ensuring the tail is to the left. Start weaving with the new strand by taking it to the back of your coil and continue wrapping and stitching as before.

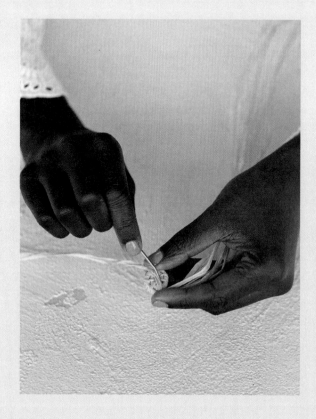

4. Shaping the basket

To shape your basket and build up the sides, place the coils directly on top of the previous round. Ensure you are holding the core material in the correct place and use each stitch to secure it. As you build up the sides, you can place the wrapped core either directly on top of the previous round for straight sides or at a slight angle for a more oval vessel.

5. Finishing touches

When you have 5cm (2 inches) of core material remaining, cut it at a 45-degree angle. Finish the basket by making stitches (no wraps) until the end of the core is concealed. Turn your work over and tie a knot. Weave the end into one of the previous stitches and cut off any excess material.

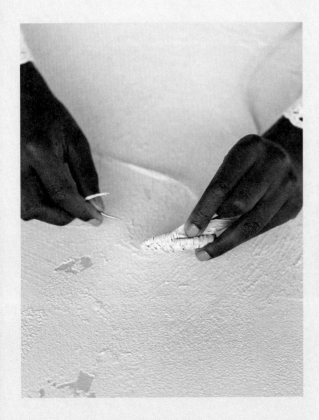

Statement earrings

I adore these statement coiled earrings, a stylish accessory to elevate any outfit all year round, and they also make a perfect gift. This is an ideal beginner project for those starting at basket-weaving – but be warned, making them becomes absolutely addictive.

Materials (for a pair of earrings)
1 hank of raffia in one colour (colour A)
5 strands of raffia in a second colour (colour B)
Long-eyed needle
Measuring tape
Scissors
Peg
Earring hooks

1. Gather 5 strands of raffia in colour A – we will refer to them as the core.

2. Grab 1 strand of raffia in colour A – we will refer to this strand as the stitching material.

3. Hold the core bundle with your left hand and, with your right hand, start wrapping the stitching material from the ends of the core, leaving a gap of 1cm (⅜ inch) at the tip, and do 5 clockwise (towards you) wraps around the core.

4. Fold the just-wrapped core into two and create a little eyelet. Wrap the stitching material around the base of the eyelet to secure it and secure with a peg.

5. Thread your needle at the other end of the stitching material and poke the needle through the central hole of the eyelet.

6. Start coiling the core into a circle, following this pattern: 4 wraps, 1 stitch.
Wrap the stitching material around the core 4 times clockwise and make 1 stitch by poking the needle in the centre of the eyelet.

7. Continue wrapping and stitching until you complete the second round of your spiral, joining the first two rounds together.

8. From now on, the stitches will always go over the current and previous rounds of your coil.

9. To join new stitching material or change colour: lay the remaining 10cm (4 inches) of colour A at the back of your coil. Take 1 new strand of raffia in the same colour and lay this at the front of your coil. Start weaving by wrapping the new strand over the core (to both secure and hide the old length) and continue with your pattern of 4 wraps and 1 stitch.

10. To add more core material when you have only 5cm (2 inches) remaining, take another 5–7 strands of raffia and wrap them around the rest of the bundle so that the 'old' core and 'new' core are both connected, and secure with a peg. Since the ends of raffia tend to be thinner and it is a flexible and pliable material, it can be easily manipulated to blend in and maintain a consistent diameter for even thickness.

11. Continue weaving with colour A until your earring reaches 7cm (2¾ inches) in diameter. Join a strand of colour B, as explained in step 9, and complete the earring with a full round of colour B.

12. Finish off the earring by covering all of the core with stitching material. Feed the needle to the back of your coil and tie a little knot. Cut off any excess materials.

13. Repeat the process to make the second earring to complete your pair.

14. Once your earrings are ready, thread each earring hook between the last and penultimate round of weaving, making sure the front of each earring is facing outwards. *Et voila*!

Raffia choker

This raffia choker pays homage to the 1990s trend that has been making a comeback in recent years. I wanted to add a playful twist to the necklace while maintaining its bohemian essence with the use of colourful raffia strands.

Materials

Cotton rope: 1m (39 inches) of cotton rope, 8mm (5/16 inch) diameter
1 hank of raffia in colour A
1 hank of raffia in colour B
Long-eyed needle
Measuring tape
Scissors
Peg
Masking tape

1. Use your measuring tape to determine the circumference of your neck and your desired fit for the choker. Once you have that number (here: 36cm/14¼ inches), double it (72cm/28½ inches), this is the length of rope needed for the project.

2. Cut the rope to the desired length and place it on your workstation. Mark the midway point (36cm/14¼ inches) with a peg.

3. Pull a long strand of raffia in colour A from the hank. Begin wrapping the raffia clockwise (towards you) around the rope, starting one thumb's width from the end.

4. Continue wrapping the raffia around the rope until you reach the peg (or midway point). If you run out of raffia before reaching the midway point, do a couple of extra wraps with the new strand over the end of the previous strand so it is secured and doesn't unravel.

5. Remove the peg, then fold the rope back on itself to create a loop. Reattach the peg to secure the loop and the raffia in place.

6. Introduce your second colour by pulling a strand of raffia in colour B from the hank and threading your needle at one end of that strand. If you have more than 10cm (4 inches) left of colour A, cut it off.

7. Holding the end of colour A so it doesn't unravel, remove the peg and join in the strand of colour B by wrapping it 4 times clockwise around 1) the end of colour A, 2) the rope, and 3) its own end to secure it.

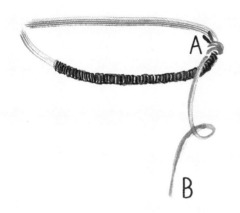

8. Make a figure-of-eight stitch: take the strand of raffia between the two halves of the loop, behind the bottom half and around it, back through the centre and behind the top half and around it to where you started.

9. Repeat by wrapping the raffia around the rope 4 times, then make another figure-of-eight, taking it around the bottom half as before. Pull gently but tightly to avoid gaps between the top and bottom halves and create a neat appearance.

10. Join in new raffia as needed – always lay the new strand at the front of your coil, ensuring the tail is to the left. Start weaving with the new strand by taking it to the back of your coil and continue wrapping and stitching as before.

11. When you have 5cm (2 inches) of rope remaining, join the two ends of the rope to create a second loop. Since the ends of the rope may have frayed, butt them together and tightly wrap a piece of masking tape around them. Continue your pattern of 4 wraps and the figure-of-eight until all the rope is covered. Thread the raffia strand under a stitch and tie a knot at the back of the choker.

12. To wear the choker, loop one long piece of raffia through each of the loops and tie a simple knot and bow at the back of your neck, or opt to let the raffia dangle down your back.

13. Ensure the knot is tight enough to secure the choker but not uncomfortable. Adjust the length by sliding the knot until the choker sits at your desired position on your neck.

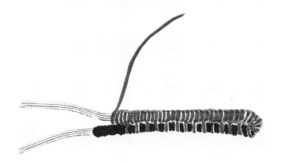

Sustainability

If you're anything like me, entering a haberdashery or craft shop is like being a kid in a candy shop. It's a magical experience, where every stack of fabric, spool of thread and roll of colourful ribbon holds the promise of some new creations and it is always very hard to leave empty handed. But in our enthusiasm for creating new and exciting projects, it's also important to consider the environmental impact of our practice and have a more mindful approach when making.

One of the mains reasons to adopt sustainable crafting practices is obviously waste reduction. The textile industry is notorious for its environmental footprint and as crafters we need to be aware that our material choices contribute to this impact. Instead of constantly purchasing new items, consider reimagining old curtains, tea towels, jeans or leftover fabric. Not only does this minimize the demand for new resources, but it also prevents these items from ending up in landfills.

Repurposing materials not only lessens waste but it also sparks creativity. Did you know you can make your own twine with some leftover fabric? Or what about replacing the cotton rope in the raffia choker (see pages 40–3) with some rolled denim?

In a world where fast fashion and disposable goods are king, choosing to repurpose and upcycle sends a strong message. It says no to throwaway culture and encourages others to consider the longevity and environmental impact of the products they ultimately buy but also make.

Three tips for sustainability

1. Responsible sourcing
Embrace natural fibres such as jute, seagrass or raffia, obtained through ethical and fair-trade suppliers. Be mindful about consumption and choose durable, long-lasting tools and accessories that won't need to be constantly replaced.

2. Embrace natural dyes
Opt for natural dyes in your projects (see pages 50–1). This choice not only adds uniqueness to your makes but also reduced the environmental impact associated with synthetic dyeing.

3. Donate to local schools
Instead of discarding your leftover materials and fabric scraps, consider donating them to local schools. Materials can often be used for patchwork, bunting and scrapbooks, allowing younger generations to fully explore their creative sides.

La petite jewellery box

Whether displayed on a dresser or tucked away in a drawer, this little box can hold your favourite sparkles or a variety of sentimental items from meaningful places and meaningful people. What treasures will yours contain?

Materials
100g (3½oz) raffia
Long-eyed needle
Scissors
Measuring tape
Peg
Optional: fabric for lining; beads, charm or brooch for embellishment

The box

1. Gather 5 long strands of raffia for the core and 1 separate strand for the stitching material. Begin making a base using a pattern of 4 wraps followed by 1 stitch until your circular coil reaches a diameter of 3cm (1¼ inches).

2. To start shaping and forming the first corner of your box, increase the number of wraps from 4 to 6. However, refrain from doing a stitch until you can gently bend the core into a square corner. Once achieved, proceed with the stitch.

3. Return to the pattern of 4 wraps and 1 stitch until you reach the next corner.

4. Repeat steps 2–3 to form the other two corners of your box base.

Note: The larger the box gets, the more defined the edges will become. As you work, regularly pause and examine the overall shape of your box. This can help you to identify and correct any misshapes before you're too far ahead.

5. Continue building the base of your square box until it measures 15 x 15cm (6 x 6 inches).

6. Now, start building the sides of the jewellery box by gradually increasing the height. Instead of working flat, position the core on top of the previous round to create straight sides. Ensure the core is in the right place, using each stitch to hold it there.

7. Continue building the sides of the box until it reaches 5cm (2 inches) in height.

8. Complete the box by doing 2 rounds going inwards (so the lid can sit securely on top). Continue stitching until you have covered all of the core. Feed the needle back through the stitches on the inside of your box, tie a little knot to secure it and trim the end.

The lid

9. Repeat the process from steps 1–5 to build a square base for your lid, measuring 15 x 15cm (6 x 6 inches). Then, build up the sides to a height of 3cm (1¼ inches), or 4 rounds. Before finishing your lid, ensure it fits on top of the box, and then complete it.

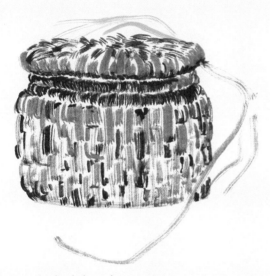

10. Finish the lid in the same way as you did the box, with stitches around the core. Feed the needle back to the inside, tie a knot and trim off any excess raffia. Secure the loose end by stitching it under the coils to maintain a neat appearance.

11. Your jewellery box is now ready for use. Consider personalizing it by adding a fabric lining, embellishing the outside with beads, or adorning the lid with a small charm or a vintage brooch.

Natural dyeing

I'll admit it, I was a late bloomer when it comes to natural dyeing. I've always been more likely to pick up a bottle of synthetic dye for convenience and speed, but in recent years (and most importantly since becoming a mother) I really swerve away from those harmful chemical concoctions.

Why run to the shops when your pantry holds the key to a breathtaking palette? It's the perfect recipe for creative magic, where spices, fruits and vegetables play the starring roles and materials such as raffia and centre cane (which, by the way, absorb and retain natural dyes beautifully) come alive in stunning new shades.

Three tips for natural dyeing

1. Pre-soak
Before dyeing, soak the raffia or centre cane in water – overnight for the raffia and for a few hours for the centre cane. This really helps the fibres to absorb the dye more evenly and deeply.

2. Use natural mordants and modifiers
Mordants and modifiers are substances that help the dye adhere to the fibres. Some common natural mordants and modifiers include citrus, vinegar and baking soda.

3. Get creative
Natural dyeing is all about experimentation and embracing the unexpected results, so open up your cupboards and don't hesitate to try different materials to achieve unique and beautiful shades.

Five everyday products for natural dyeing

1. Tea bags
This was the first product I experimented with as I go through five cuppas a day and I just love the natural brown shade it gives to my creations (see page 130).

2. Onion skins
Save those papery outer skins of yellow or red onions and boil them to create beautiful shades of yellow and orange.

3. Avocado pits and skins
The pits and skins of avocados can produce soft pink and peachy tones. Simmer them to release the dye.

4. Turmeric
This vibrant spice will give your projects yellow tones. Be cautious as turmeric can stain, so handle it with care.

5. Spinach
This leafy green vegetable can yield delicate green shades. It's perfect for a more subtle and earthy colour palette.

Raffia mini bag

This mini bag pays homage to my iconic 'Rope Basket Bag', which has become the epitome of my style and is probably one of my most sought-after projects. Numerous requests for a sewing-machine-free version inspired this design – and here it is! A petite bag, ideal for carrying just the essentials, whether you're heading out for a casual lunch or a more sophisticated evening soirée.

Materials
200g (7oz) raffia
Long-eyed needle
Scissors
Pins
Ruler or measuring tape
Optional: extra-strong thread

1. Gather 5 strands of raffia to form a bundle (the core) and use 1 single piece of raffia for stitching (the stitching material).

2. Begin wrapping the single piece of raffia clockwise (towards you) around the bundle, starting one thumb's width from the end. Aim for approximately 5–6 wraps, ensuring you can fold the covered core to create a small eyelet. Make sure both sides are covered with the stitching material. Wrap the stitching material around the base of the eyelet.

3. Thread your needle onto the opposite end of the stitching material and insert the needle through the central hole of the eyelet.

4. Start coiling the bundle into a circle, following this pattern: wrap the stitching material clockwise (towards you) around the bundle for approximately 1cm (⅜ inch) or 4–5 wraps, and stitch by inserting your needle through the central hole of the eyelet. Repeat until you have completed a full round.

5. Continue with the same pattern of wrapping and stitching, ensuring the stitches overlap the current and previous rounds of your coil (one row below).

6. As you continue with the same pattern, ensure your base remains flat. Join in new core material and new stitching material when appropriate (when you have only 5cm/2 inches of core material left – see page 34 for instructions).

7. When your coil has reached a diameter of 18cm (7 inches), pause, making sure that you do so after completing a stitch and not mid-wrap.

8. It's time to add your handle. For my mini bag, I chose a narrow handle close to my wrist, but this is entirely your own style decision. Fold your coil in half and measure 14cm (5½ inches) from the fold. Mark this point with a pin on each half. This is where your handle will start and end (feel free to adjust this according to your own style decision).

9. Start wrapping the stitching material around the core from the first pin to the second one – this will give your handle some sturdiness. Once you've reached the second pin and you're happy with the length of the handle, secure the stitching material by doing a stitch one row below – as you've done throughout the project.

10. Restart your coiling pattern of wrapping and stitching around the lower part of the coil, going from one end of the handle (pin 2) until you're back at the other (pin 1).

11. To build up the sides of your bag (to give the finished bag depth), loop the core bundle back on itself and start wrapping and stitching in the opposite direction all around the lower part of the coil until you reach the other end of the handle (pin 1 to pin 2).

12. Repeat this until you have extended the width by 2 loops beyond the handle on one side and 1 loop on the other side. You have now completed the first half of your bag.

13. Repeat steps 1–12 to create the second half of your bag and its handle.

14. Match the 2-looped side on your first half of the bag with the 1-looped side on the second half and hand stitch the two sides together with a piece of raffia or some extra-strong thread.

Cane

Cane

Cane baskets are essentials in modern homes, effortlessly merging practicality with natural charm. Their versatile appeal ensures they find a place in every room, enhancing decor with their creamy hues and intricate weaves. Sourced from the inner core of the rattan palm thriving in the wilds of tropical regions, the finest quality cane originates primarily from Southeast Asia.

Once harvested, cane undergoes a meticulous transformation process, shedding its outer layer adorned with prickly thorns before being split into various thicknesses. Available in reels measured by weight, centre cane offers a diverse range of sizes to cater to a wide range of projects (please see the size chart on page 22 for guidance on the sizes used in this book).

Working with centre cane is commonly known as 'stake and strand' – initially weaving the flat base (or 'slath', see page 60) with horizontal 'strands', followed by attaching vertical 'stakes' to form the structure of the sides. Once the sides

are woven, these stakes are used to create the border at the top (see the detailed step-by-step photos on pages 60–65).

When looping a piece of cane around your slath to start weaving, you'll find yourself with two weavers, one on each side of your stakes – these are commonly referred to as the left-hand weaver (positioned on your left) and the right-hand weaver (positioned on your right).

To prepare cane for weaving, soaking it in lukewarm water is essential, enhancing its flexibility and ensuring smooth manipulation. And if you do find yourself wrestling with a "reluctant" bundle, remember the golden rule: when in doubt, let it soak a tad longer while you sneak off for a quick tea break. Who knows, maybe by the time you return, the cane will be feeling more cooperative, or at least you'll have had a refreshing cuppa to ease the frustration!

How-to

This section will guide you through the basics of creating a stake-and-strand basket using centre cane with a round base. The process includes weaving a base, joining new stakes, and shaping and creating a border. This method and technique will prove invaluable throughout your basketry journey, allowing you to explore your creativity.

For more guidance mastering this basketry technique, watch a comprehensive video tutorial featuring essential steps along with helpful tips at www.labasketry.com/pages/woven.

Materials
6 x 30cm (24 inches) of 3.00mm (⅛ inch) centre cane for the stakes
3 lengths of 2.65mm (⁷⁄₆₄ inch) centre cane for the weavers
Cane cutters
Measuring tape
Bodkin
Pliers
Bowl of lukewarm water
Hand towel

1. Making a slath

The starting point for all cane baskets is making a slath. Use cane cutters to cut 6 lengths of centre cane. To create a 3-through-3 slath using your bodkin, group the stakes into 2 sets of 3. Begin by piercing through the middle of 1 stake with your bodkin.

2.

Repeat the process with the next 2 stakes, resulting in a total of 3 pierced stakes.

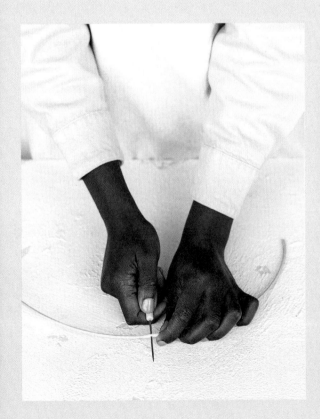

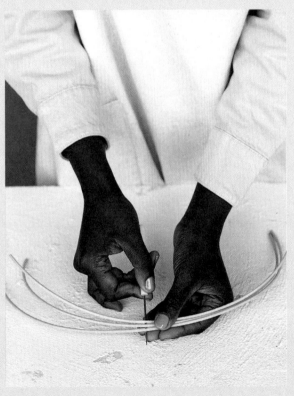

3.

Insert the remaining 3 unpierced stakes through the 3 pierced ones to form a cross. (Note: You may encounter projects that require a 4-through-4 slath or a 6-through-6 slath – the number of stakes may change but the method remains the same.)

4. Weaving the base

Soak a couple of bundles of cane in a bucket of lukewarm water for 15 minutes.

Loop 1 length of cane over 3 of the stakes and pull it down until it sits next to the crossed pieces. Hold down the right-hand weaver with your left thumb and guide the left-hand weaver in front of the first group of 3 stakes (group 1) and behind the next group of stakes (group 2).

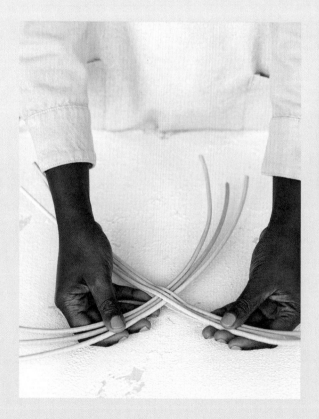

Pull tightly, then rotate the slath a quarter anti-clockwise so that the left-hand weaver becomes the right-hand weaver.

Continue rotating the slath a quarter anti-clockwise and repeating the process: hold the right-hand weaver and guide the left-hand weaver in front of (group 2) and behind (group 3), then in front of (group 3) and behind (group 4), and finally in front of (group 4) and behind (group 1).

Tip: You always want your stakes to be a thicker cane than your weavers.

5.

After completing a full round, continue by repeating this weaving technique, called 'pairing' (in front, behind, in front, behind), for a second round.

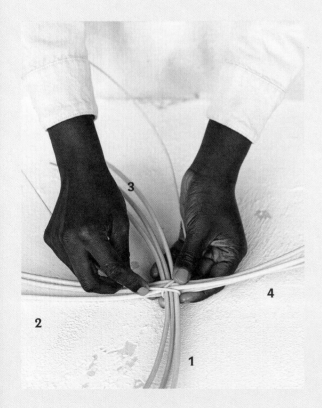

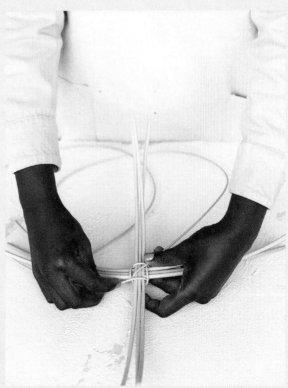

6.

Begin separating the stakes (currently grouped into sets of 3) into individual stakes using the same pairing technique, but now weaving in front of one stake and behind another.

Pull the stakes apart slightly, allowing the weaving to go down into the spaces between the stakes to ensure tightness. Re-soak the cane if it doesn't feel flexible enough, and strive to keep the stakes evenly spaced.

7. Shaping the sides

When the base reaches the desired size, shape the sides of the basket by adding new stakes turned up vertically. To do this, cut new stakes with your cutters, insert them to the right of your base stakes, using the bodkin to create space.

Allow them to soak for a few minutes, then use pliers to pinch each stake at the base and bend it upwards.

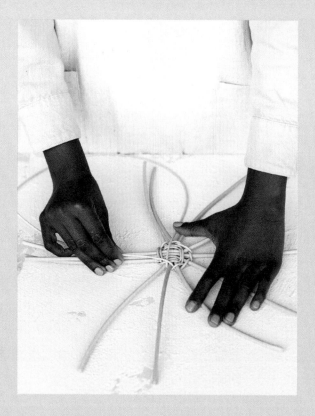

8. Finishing off

Once the basket has reached the desired height, soak the stakes for 5–10 minutes. Then, using pliers, pinch each stake where you've finished weaving to fold it to the right

Select 1 stake, pull it in front of the stake to its right and cross that stake over it to the front, then in turn bring that stake in front of the one to its right, and so on. Repeat this process for each stake, weaving to the front until a full row is complete. Trim the ends evenly but avoid cutting them too short as that may cause the rim to come undone.

How to join a new weaver

When your left-hand weaver is around 5cm (2 inches) short, it's time to join a new weaver. Place the end of the new weaver alongside the end of the previous one, overlapping them by 10cm (4 inches). Hold the overlapping ends firmly together and restart weaving with the new weaver.

Once you've completed a full round and returned to the overlap, trim off the end of the previous weaver so it lies over a stake.

Knotmark

Say goodbye to folded corners and frantic page searching. This cane bookmark is such a fun little make and the perfect introductory project to working with centre cane – soaking, twisting and looping. Once you've mastered the technique, a world of inspiring creations unfolds before you, with endless possibilities to explore.

Materials
2 x 60cm (23½ inches) of 2.5mm (³⁄₃₂ inches) centre cane
Cane cutters
Ruler or measuring tape
Bowl of lukewarm water
Hand towel
Ribbon, string or thread of your choice

1. Begin by cutting 2 lengths of centre cane to 60cm (23½ inches) and immersing them in lukewarm water for 15–20 minutes, allowing them to become fully pliable.

2. Working on a flat surface, align the 2 cane pieces and measure 20cm (8 inches) from the left end. Mark this point with your thumb – this is where you want to do your first loop.

Take the left end of the canes and loop them over the right ends to form a loop with a diameter of approximately 3.5cm (1⅜ inches) – this is loop 1.

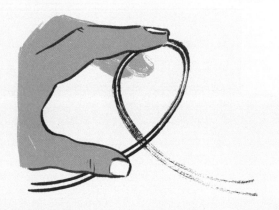

3. Shape your second loop (loop 2) using the same ends of the cane pieces which are still the left ones, mirroring the first loop. The bookmark should take on an almost heart-like appearance, with two half loops meeting in the centre. Ensure that loop 1 and loop 2 are of a similar size.

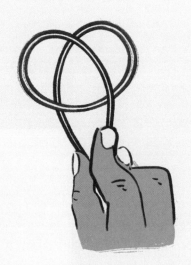

4. For loop 3, pass the cane ends of loop 2 under the ends of loop 1, holding them at this point with your other hand, and thread them inside loop 2.

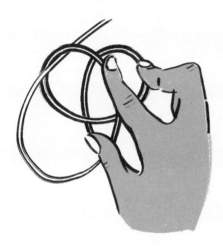

5. As you work, ensure the cane stays flexible by regularly soaking it for a few minutes to prevent it from snapping. Readjust your loops to maintain alignment and ensure that all 3 loops are a similar size.

6. Take the ends of loop 3 and bring them to the front by threading them through the 2 loops in front of them. They should now sit at the front of your make.

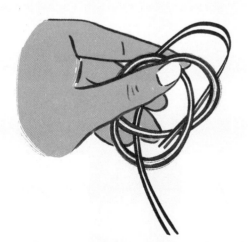

7. Re-soak for 5 minutes and then readjust the loops, so they are all a similar size, by pulling the ends of the pieces of cane.

8. Finish by creating loop 4 – take the ends of loop 3 and fold them back onto themselves, then thread them through loop 1. The ends should now sit at the back of your make.

9. Readjust the loops once more so they are all of a similar size, then securely tie the ends of loop 4, which sit at the back, together with the ends of loop 1, which sit at the front, using one piece of string at the top and a second piece of string closer to the ends, and trim the ends to the same length.

10. Now, unleash your creativity! These knotmarks are perfect for your reading experience but also serve as charming additions to your dinner party table settings. Explore the endless possibilities that unfold once you've mastered this technique.

Bangle

Whether you wear just one for a touch of boho chic or stack up a few to make a bold statement, these rattan bangles are so striking and so addictive to make. I found my inspiration for them in the chunky wooden bangles I used to buy in the vibrant markets of Dakar and eagerly bring back for my girlfriends and myself. The louder the clink, the more cherished the memories they hold.

Materials

70cm (27½ inches) of 2.5mm (³⁄₃₂ inch) centre cane for the stakes
2 lengths of 2.00mm (⁵⁄₆₄ inch) centre cane for the weavers
Measuring tape
Cane cutters
Masking tape
Clips
Bowl of lukewarm water
Hand towel
Rubber bands
Optional: varnish or sealant and brush

1. Using a measuring tape, determine and mark your preferred bangle length. Take into account the circumference of your wrist (mine is 18cm/7 inches) and add 5–7cm (2–2¾ inches) for a loose fit and ease of putting it on, totalling 23cm (9 inches).

2. Carefully cut 3 lengths of cane from the 2.5mm (3⁄32 inch) centre cane, each measuring 23cm (9 inches). These will serve as the stakes for your project.

3. Lay the 3 stakes on a flat surface, spaced 2cm (¾ inch) apart. Measure 5cm (2 inches) at the bottom of the stakes and secure them in place using masking tape or clips to maintain straight alignment with consistent gaps.

4. Immerse a length of 2.00mm (5⁄64 inch) cane in lukewarm water for 10 minutes (until it becomes flexible enough to work with).

5. Begin weaving at the 5cm (2 inches) point of your stakes. Position your weaver (the length of cane you soaked in step 4) to the left of the left stake. Weave it in front of the left stake, behind the middle stake, and then in front of the right stake.

6. Flip your project over and repeat the weaving process, moving from left to right. Weave in front of the left stake, behind the middle stake, and then in front of the right stake.

7. Re-soak your stakes and the weaver if needed – you might need to keep holding them while they are submerged in the water so the weaving doesn't unravel at this stage.

8. Continue alternating sides and weave around your stakes until you have about 10cm (4 inches) left at the top.

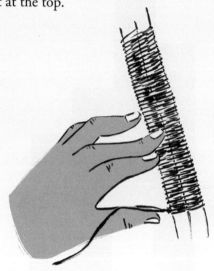

9. Soak your make for 10–15 minutes – don't hesitate to refresh the water if it has become too cold. You want the cane to be able to bend without snapping.

10. Carefully bend the cane into a circular shape, matching the top and bottom ends of each stake and overlapping them, tucking the tips into the weaving on the opposite ends.

11. Hold the circular shape in place using clips, masking tape or rubber bands.

12. Resume weaving the last 15cm (6 inches) of the bangle, repeating the weaving technique from steps 5–6. Remove the clips, masking tape or rubber band as you progress.

13. To finish the bangle and prevent it from unravelling, thread the weaver back through the middle stake.

14. Trim any excess length using cane cutters.

15. Optionally, apply a thin coat of varnish or sealant and allow it to dry completely before wearing your bangle.

Tip: Experiment with different thicknesses of cane (stakes and weavers) to create varied bangle styles – just change the space between the stakes in step 3 to do so.

Cane mirror

Mirror, mirror on the wall, who's woven this beauty, adorning the hall? I started this project with my daughter's nursery in mind. You know how toddlers are obsessed with their reflections? The plan was a cute little mirror for her room, but guess what? It ended up claiming another corner of the house. Perfect for those mad dashes out of the door when you just need a quick peek at yourself.

Materials

Round wooden basket base with 26 holes, 17.5cm (7 inches) in diameter
Round mirror, 15cm (6 inches) in diameter (make sure the mirror is smaller than the wooden base you work with)
200g (7oz) of 2.65mm (7/64 inch) centre cane
30g (1oz) of 2.00mm (5/64 inch) centre cane
Wood glue
Measuring tape
Cane cutters
Bodkin
Bucket of lukewarm water
Hand towel
Pencil
Spray water bottle
Microfibre cloth

The base

1. Begin by applying wood glue to the back of the mirror and positioning it centrally on the basket base. Press down firmly to ensure a strong bond with the base. Allow the wood glue to dry completely by leaving it overnight.

2. The next day, cut 26 stakes of 2.65mm (7/64 inch) cane (matching the number of holes on your wooden base), each measuring 80cm (31½ inches).

Note: When purchasing a basket base, the size of the centre cane it accommodates should be stated – the base used here takes centre cane up to 3.00mm (⅛ inch) in diameter. If necessary, you can use a bodkin to enlarge the holes.

Tip: For efficiency, use your measuring tape to accurately cut the first stake to the required length, then use this stake as a guide to cut and measure the remaining stakes in bundles of five.

3. Soak your stakes and a couple of bundles of 2.00mm (5/64 inch) cane in lukewarm water for about 10 minutes.

4. In the meantime, mark each hole from 1–26 on the back of the wooden base with a pencil. These will be referenced as hole 1, hole 2, hole 3, and so on, throughout this project.

5. Take 1 freshly soaked stake and push one end through hole 1 to the front of the base. Then push the other end of the same stake through hole 2 to the front of the base. Pull each end back and forth until they are the same length.

6. Grab your next stake and push one end through hole 2 and the hole to its right, hole 3, again making sure the ends are the same length on either side. You'll start to notice that each hole has 2 stakes.

7. Going around your base, repeat steps 5–6: the next stake will be pulled through hole 3 and hole 4, and the one after through hole 4 and hole 5.

8. By the end, you should have 52 stakes, each approximately 40cm (15¾ inches) long.

The weaving

9. Starting at hole 1, begin weaving around the mirror using a bundle of pre-soaked 2.00mm (⁵⁄₆₄ inch) cane, working 2 rounds of pairing (in front of two stakes and behind two stakes – see steps 4–5, page 62–3).

10. Re-soak the stakes before starting the decorative border. However, be cautious not to soak the mirror itself, as this may weaken the glue; instead, use a spray water bottle to wet the stakes at the base.

11. Starting at hole 1, bend the 2 stakes behind the ones at hole 2 and in front of the next 2 stakes at hole 3. Hold them down.

12. Now working with the 2 stakes at hole 2, bend them and place them behind the 2 new upright stakes at hole 3, and in front of the 2 new stakes at hole 4. Hold them down.

Tip: The trick here is to work outwards – away from the mirror and not on top of the round of pairing you did in step 9 – as you want your border to sit along the wooden base.

13. Repeat this sequence, working with the stakes at each hole, going around twice until you have completed 2 full rounds.

14. Cut the ends, ensuring they lie behind a stake. Avoid cutting them too short to prevent the cane from unravelling.

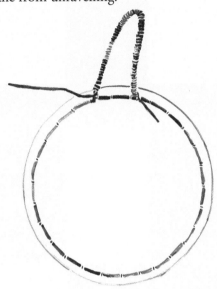

15. To hang the mirror, begin by cutting a 30cm (12 inch) length from the 2.65mm (⁷⁄₆₄ inch) cane bundle. Soak this piece in water for 5 minutes. Next, loop it under 2 returns of the stakes located on the back of the wooden base. This will create a reversed U-shaped loop that is 8cm (3¼ inches) tall.

Now, working from left to right, take the end of the cane on the left side and wrap it around the loop until you reach the right side. Then, thread it under the return and trim off any excess cane. You now have a small loop suitable for hanging the mirror on a wall.

16. Use a microfibre cloth and a spray of water to clean the mirror, and it's ready to be hung.

Flower basket bag

Ideal for carrying your freshly picked blooms from the Sunday flower market, this basket bag effortlessly combines practicality with style.
It would work brilliantly as a chic bottle carrier for a picnic, or why not remove the strap and use it as a vase on a mantelpiece?

Materials
100g (3½oz) of 2.5mm (³⁄₃₂ inch) centre cane for the stakes
50g (2oz) of 2.00mm (⁵⁄₆₄ inch) centre cane for the weavers
Measuring tape
Cane cutters
Bucket of lukewarm water
Hand towel
Bodkin
Piece of ribbon or twine, or a rubber band
Pliers
Weight
Detachable leather strap with clasps

The base

1. Cut 12 pieces of 2.5mm (³⁄₃₂ inch) cane to 1m (39 inches) in length for your base stakes and make a 6-through-6 slath (see steps 1–3, page 61). Submerge your slath and a couple of bundles of 2.00mm (⁵⁄₆₄ inch) cane in lukewarm water for 15 minutes.

2. Begin tightly weaving your base with 2 rounds of pairing, using the freshly soaked 2.00mm (⁵⁄₆₄ inch) cane (see steps 4–5, pages 62–3).

3. Begin separating the stakes, which are currently grouped into sets of 6, into groups of 2 stakes, using the same pairing technique but now weaving in front of 2 stakes and behind 2 stakes for 3 rounds.

4. Now add more stakes – cut 2 additional stakes of 50cm (19¾ inches) for each existing one (totalling 24 stakes) from the 2.5mm (³⁄₃₂ inch) bundle. Using a bodkin to widen the space, insert 1 new stake on both sides of every base stake, 1 to the left of it and 1 to the right of it.

5. Ensure a sturdy base by working 4 rounds of pairings – weaving in front of 4 stakes (2 of the initial base stakes and 2 of the stakes added in step 4) and behind 4 stakes.

6. Separate the group of 4 stakes into 2 by working in front of 2 stakes and behind 2 stakes for the next 5 rounds. Maintain an even space between each pair of stakes, resulting in a base diameter of 13cm (5 inches).

The sides

7. Securely tie the pairs of stakes together with ribbon or twine, and soak the base in water for 10–15 minutes before commencing to build the bag's sides.

8. Using pliers, bend the stakes at the base to start shaping upwards. Work on a flat surface, and use a weight to keep the base flat.

9. Continue weaving with 8 rounds of pairing (going in front of 2 stakes and behind 2 stakes) using freshly soaked 2.00mm (⁵⁄₆₄ inch) cane. After the 8th row, trim off the weavers and tuck the ends under the last round.

10. Leave a 4cm (1⅝ inch) gap and re-loop one bundle of 2.00mm (⁵⁄₆₄ inch) cane over the stakes, then proceed with another 8 rounds of pairing.

11. After completing the 8th round, leave another 4cm (1⅝ inch) gap before restarting the weaving.

12. Repeat steps 10–11 until you have 4 sets of 8 rounds of pairings, leaving 4 gaps of 4cm (1⅝ inches); your basket should now measure 32cm (12½ inches) tall.

13. Weave 4 additional rounds of pairings.

The border

14. Re-soak the stakes for 10–15 minutes before finishing your bag. Take 2 stakes (stakes A), place them behind the next 2 upright stakes (stakes B), and in front of the next 2 stakes (stakes C). Hold down stakes A.

15. Take stakes B, place them behind the next 2 upright stakes (stakes C), and in front of the next 2 stakes (stakes D). Hold down stakes B.

16. Repeat this sequence until all the stakes are threaded on the inside. Trim any excess cane on the inside of the base.

17. Clip on your leather strap – your stylish bag is ready to use.

Criss-cross basket bag

This project is a fun take on a classic ladylike handheld bag, featuring a playful criss-cross pattern and a contrasting coloured lining. It has an oval base, which is a little more advanced to make than a round one, so take your time before tackling this project and make sure you've had a lot of practice making round bases and familiarizing yourself with the terminology and the intricacies of working with centre cane.

Materials

100g (3½oz) of 2.5mm (²⁄₃₂ inch) centre cane for the stakes
50g (2oz) of 2.00mm (⁵⁄₆₄ inch) centre cane for the weavers
Measuring tape
Cane cutters
Bodkin
Bucket of lukewarm water
Hand towel
Pliers
Weight
Pegs

For the lining

Fabric of your choice
Matching sewing thread
Scissors
Iron and ironing board
Pins
Sewing machine
Needle

The base

1. First cut 18 stakes of 2.5mm (³⁄₃₂ inch) cane to 1m (39 inches) in length. These will be used to make a 6-through-12 slath (see steps 1–3, page 61).

2. To make a 6-through-12 slath, start by gathering the stakes into 2 groups: 1 set of 6 and 1 set of 12. Begin by piercing through the middle of each of the 12 stakes using a bodkin. Then, insert the 6 unpierced stakes through the pierced ones. Arrange the 12 stakes into 6 pairs of 2, leaving gaps of 3cm (1¼ inches) between each pair. The 12 stakes represent the length of the bag, while the 6 stakes represent its width.

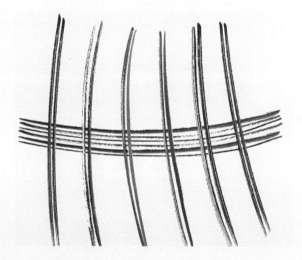

3. Soak your slath and a couple of bundles of 2.00mm (⁵⁄₆₄ inch) cane in lukewarm water for 15 minutes.

4. Loop a length of cane over of a pair of stakes and start your base working 3 rounds of pairing weaving, going in front of a pair of stakes then behind a pair of stakes (see steps 4–5, pages 62–3). Repeat 6 times until you get to the side of your slath, where you'll work in front of the 6 stakes and then behind a pair of stakes.

5. On round 4, open the side stakes (the group of 6) into 3 pairs of 2 stakes for 2 rounds.

6. It's time to add some stakes to strengthen your base. Cut 36 pieces of 2.5mm (³⁄₃₂ inch) centre cane to 60cm (23½ inches) in length. Using your bodkin, insert 1 stake to the left and 1 to the right of each pair of stakes, so each pair is now a group of 4 stakes.

7. Soak your base in lukewarm water for 5–10 minutes and work another 3 rounds of pairing (going in front of 4 stakes, behind 4 stakes). The base of your basket bag should now measure about 26cm (10¼ inches) in width – it's time to build the sides of your bag.

The sides

8. Using your pliers, bend the stakes upwards so you can start shaping the bag. Continue with rounds of pairing for another 10 rounds (in front of 4 stakes, behind 4 stakes). Don't hesitate to use a weight to keep your base flat as you start to go up.

9. Start the criss-cross pattern. Working from left to right, separate a group of 4 stakes into 2 groups of 2 stakes (your 2 left stakes and your 2 right stakes). Take your 2 right stakes and cross them behind the 2 stakes to their right, creating an inverted V. Use a peg to hold them in place. Each opening should be approximately 5cm (2 inches) in height.

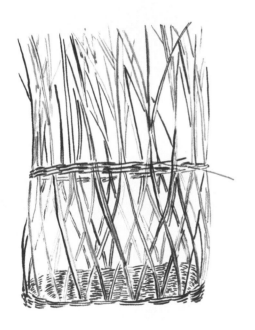

10. Take the next 2 stakes and cross them behind the 2 stakes to their right. Hold them in place with a peg.

11. Repeat until all the stakes have been crossed to create the intricate pattern of the bag.

12. Measure 12cm (4¾ inches) in height from your last round of pairing – this is where you want to restart weaving the bag.

13. Soak your stakes again for 10–15 minutes and restart by working in rounds of pairing. Loop a length of cane over 4 stakes and weave in front of 4 stakes and behind 4 stakes for 10 rounds.

14. Before beginning the border, trim the 2 right stakes from each group of 4 stakes, leaving only 2 stakes remaining in each group.

15. Thread a pair of stakes through the pair of stakes on its right, and repeat until all stakes have been threaded through (see step 9, page 65). Trim any excess cane that doesn't lie flat against the basket.

The handles

16. To make your first handle, cut two lengths of 2.00mm (5/64 inch) cane, each measuring 1.2m (47¼ inches), and soak them for 15 minutes.

17. While the cane soaks, measure 12cm (4¾ inches) from one side of the bag to the centre of the bag and mark this point (point A) with a peg – this is where your handle will start. Then, measure 10cm (4 inches) from point A and mark this point (point B) with another peg – this will be where the handle ends.

18. Starting from point A, count down 5 rounds and insert one end of each of the 2 soaked pieces of cane through the front of the bag, pulling them halfway through. Gather the 4 ends of the cane lengths together above the bag's border.

19. At point B, count down 5 rounds and insert the same 4 ends of the cane from the front of the bag to create a handle from point A to point B. Pull the ends through on the inside of the bag until the external handle measures 20cm (8 inches).

20. Working anti-clockwise, start wrapping the 4 lengths around the handle from point B to point A.

21. When you've reached point A, insert the 4 ends at the 5-round gap where you started in Step 18, and pull them tightly from the front of the bag to the inside of the bag. Thread the ends into the weaving of one of the previous rounds to secure them and cut off any excess cane.

22. Repeat steps 16–21 to make a matching handle on the other side of the bag.

The lining

23. Cut 2 pieces of your fabric, each measuring 34 x 28cm (13½ x 11 inches).

24. Iron both pieces to remove any wrinkles and ensure a smooth surface for sewing.

25. Place them right sides together and pin along the sides and bottom, leaving the top open. Using a sewing machine, sew along the pinned edges with a 1.5cm (½ inch) seam allowance.

26. With the iron, press the seams open and press the raw edges over by 1.5cm (½ inch). Drop the lining into the bag and, using a needle and thread, hand sew the folded top edge to it, just below the border you've woven in step 15, (see page 85). The thread should go over the stakes and never over the weaving, ensuring the stitches are hidden.

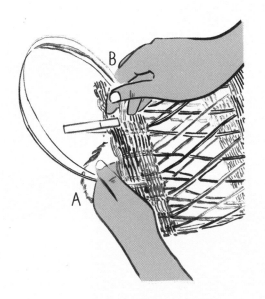

Personalize your basket bags

My love for basket bags knows no bounds, but what's even more enjoyable to me is customizing them to reflect my own style and personality. Here are some tips to take your basket bags from ordinary to extraordinary.

1. Paint
Unleash your inner Van Gogh by painting your basket bag with vibrant colours and designs. Use acrylic paints, which adhere well to straw or rattan, and sketch your ideas lightly with a pencil before adding a rainbow of colours.

2. Embroidery
Whether it's delicate flowers, initials or more intricate patterns, embroidery easily elevates any woven accessories. Use a disappearing ink pen to lightly sketch the outline of your design. Before starting on your actual bag, practise basic embroidery stitches on a scrap of fabric. I love experimenting with layering different stitches to add texture to the patterns I usually embroider.

3. Tassels and pompoms
Use pre-made tassels or craft your own with yarn, embroidery floss or even some leftover raffia from one of your projects. Attach them to the bag's handles or edges and don't forget to play around with various lengths and colours. Tassels and pompoms not only catch the eye but also add a bohemian charm that will set your bag apart.

4. Beads
Friendship bracelets have made a comeback, so why not give your bags the beaded treatment? Select beads in different shapes and sizes and weave them through the core of your bag to create patterns, or simply add them to the handles.

5. Accessorize with scarves
Choose a scarf that complements the style of your bag and tie it onto the handle, letting the ends hang down. You can also fold the scarf and tuck it inside the bag, ensuring it pokes out slightly to create a peekaboo effect. Whenever you're ready for a change, just undo the scarf and tie it in your hair or around your neck instead.

Braiding

Braiding

As a black woman, braiding has always held a special place in my heart. I vividly remember sitting between my mother's legs as a child, feeling the gentle tug of her fingers weaving intricate patterns into my hair. It wasn't just about style, it was a ritual and a connection to my heritage that I instinctively understood from a young age.

This deep-rooted connection likely explains why I have such a profound affinity with braiding (or plaiting): a basketry technique used to create long strips that can then be sewn into an array of practical and decorative items, from bags to hats.

While many of you are already familiar with the basic 3-strand braid commonly used for hair, the beauty of braiding lies in its versatility. By working with more bundles, you can create wider braids, opening up endless possibilities for creativity (see pages 96–103).

In the projects featured in this section, raffia takes centre stage, but once you've mastered the fundamentals, you can explore braiding with fabric strips, plant materials, rope, ribbons, or even use it to add a touch of je ne sais quoi to your culinary creations, like decorating a tart with braided pastry dough. The only limit is your imagination.

How-to

This section will guide you through some of the basics of plaiting (often known as braiding) with raffia, including how to make a 3-strand, 4-strand and 5-strand braid, how to start your woven project, stitching and finishing.

For more guidance mastering this basketry technique, watch a comprehensive video tutorial featuring essential steps along with helpful tips at www.labasketry.com/pages/woven.

You will need
1 hank of raffia
Masking tape or weight
Measuring tape
Scissors
Long-eyed needle

How to make a 3-strand braid

1.

Divide the bundle of raffia into 3 groups of 3 for a 3-strand braid, labelling each group bundle 1, bundle 2 and bundle 3. Lay the bundles side by side.

Tip: Secure the raffia to your work surface using masking tape or use a small weight to keep the braid steady and prevent it from moving.

2.

Take the middle group (bundle 2) and cross it over the right group (bundle 3).

3.

Now, take the right group (bundle 3) and cross it over the left group (bundle 1).

4.

Repeat steps 2 and 3 until your braid is the desired length.

How to make a 4-strand braid

1.

Divide the strands into 4 groups of 4 for a 4-strand braid, numbered 4–1 from the outer left to the outer right. Lay the groups side by side.

2.

Take the outermost right bundle (bundle 1) and cross it over the one to its left (bundle 2) and behind (bundle 3), creating the sequence 4, 1, 3, 2.

3.

Next, take the outermost left bundle (bundle 4) and cross it behind the one to its right and over the next one.

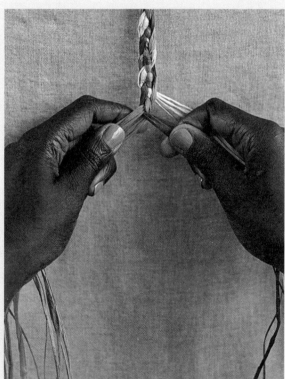

4.

Continue braiding by repeating steps 2 and 3, ensuring a flat braid. Use a weight to flatten the braid as it grows in length.

How to make a 5-strand braid

1.

Divide the strands into 5 groups for a 5-strand braid, numbered from 5–1 (moving from the outer left to the outer right in the sequence: 5, 4, 3, 2, 1). Lay the groups side by side.

2.

Keep the 5 bundles separate, forming 2 groups: bundle 5 and bundle 4 together, and bundle 3, bundle 2 and bundle 1 together. Always maintain 2 groups – one with 2 bundles and the other with 3 bundles. Start braiding from the group with the most bundles.

3.

Cross the outermost right bundle (bundle 1) over bundle 2 and then behind bundle 3 to join bundle 5 and bundle 4.

Note: If renumbering the bundles in a descending sequence, bundle 1 now becomes bundle 3.

4.

Ensure the 5 bundles are separate, grouping bundle 1, bundle 2 and bundle 3 together, and bundle 4 and bundle 5 together.

5.

Cross the outermost left bundle (bundle 5) over bundle 4 and then behind bundle 3, joining bundle 2 and bundle 1.

6.

Repeat steps 3–5, alternating between the right and left sides. Pull the strands tightly to keep the braid tight, working flat. Use a weight to flatten the braid if needed.

How to make a braided coaster using a 4-strand braid

1.

Gather your strands of raffia and tie them together at one end with an additional strand. Secure them on a flat surface with a piece of masking tape or a weight so they don't move as you start to braid.

2. Starting the 4-strand braid

Divide the bundle into 4 groups of 4 for a 4-strand braid and start braiding. (See pages 98–100 for the full process of making a 4-strand braid.)

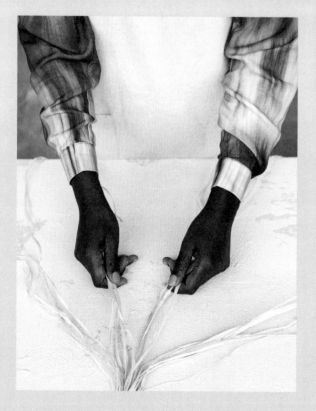
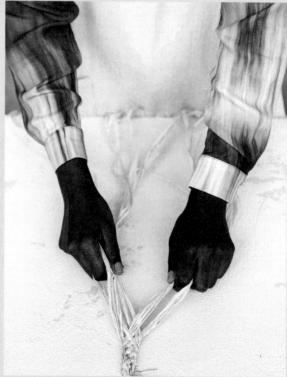

3. Joining in new raffia

As a natural material, raffia can vary in length within the same package, depending on how it has been processed and packed. In addition, the ends of the strands are often thinner due to the structure of the palm leaves from which it is derived. Therefore, you may need to join in new raffia at different stages during your project, aiming to keep the thickness as consistent as possible.

When a group of raffia strands starts to thin out, lay new strands on top of the thinning group, leaving ends of approximately 5–7cm (2–2¾ inches). Use a weight to firmly hold the new strands and the thinning group in place as you resume braiding. As your braid gets longer, adjust the position of the weight to maintain consistent pressure along the length of the braid.

4. Finishing the braid

When your braid has reached your desired length, secure the end by tying a knot with a new piece of raffia – hold the braid down with a weight while you do this to prevent it from unravelling. Trim any loose ends to tidy up the braid.

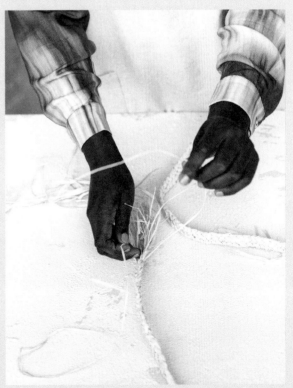

5. Stitching the braid

Thread 1 strand of raffia into your long-eyed needle to start stitching.

6.

Loop the end of your braid (about 1cm/ ⅜ inch) under. Begin coiling the braid anti-clockwise until you form a flat circle with a diameter of 3cm (1¼ inches).

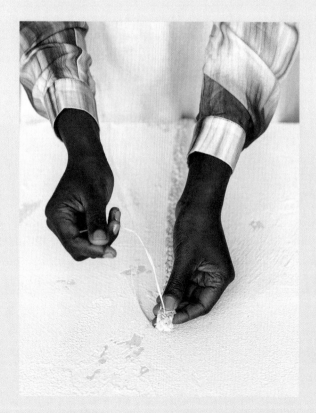

Tip: To prevent the needle from slipping out while stitching, you can tie a small knot close to the eye of your needle. Ensure that the knot is small enough to pass through the raffia easily as you stitch.

7.

Start stitching from the back by threading the stitching material through the central hole and tying a knot at the back to secure it. Guide the needle through 2 layers of braid, slanting the stitches from right to left to conceal them as much as possible.

8.

Join new stitching material by knotting the piece that's running out to the new piece, and continue the stitching pattern.

Tip: Regularly check your base and lay it on your work surface to ensure it stays level. If you notice any areas where the base begins to curve upwards, gently press down on those sections to flatten them.

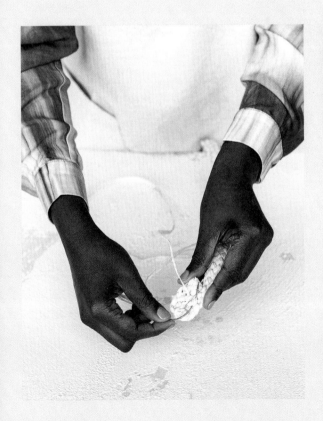

9.

Continue coiling the braid into a circle until it reaches the required size.

10. Finishing off the coaster

Finish off by gradually sewing the braid into the row below. Tie a knot to secure your last stitch and trim off the end to neaten.

How to make a mould

For some projects in this chapter you'll need to craft a cardboard mould. You'll use this to wrap your braided raffia around, to shape and build the sides of your bags. The mould functions as a support structure (you're not tightly wrapping and stitching around it), allowing flexibility and adjustments as you progress.

Each bag mould consists of five panels: a front, a back, a base and two sides. These panels can be crafted from various types of cardboard that you probably already have at home (such as discarded packaging material), simply by measuring, cutting, folding and assembling with adhesive tape.

Sizing considerations

Factoring in the additional thickness of the braided raffia, the mould should be slightly smaller than the desired final dimensions of your project. This also ensures it is easy to remove without distorting or damaging your make at the end.

Determining a mould's dimensions

Use the width of your braid as a reference. See the following examples:

If your 4-strand braid measures 3cm (1¼ inches) in width, and the base of your bag is 15 x 9cm (6 x 3½ inches), deduct the width of the braid and the base panel you need for your mould would be 12 x 6cm (4¾ x 2¼ inches).

If your 3-strand braid measures 2cm (¾ inch) in width, and the base of your bag is 20 x 30cm (8 x 12 inches), deduct the width of the braid and, in this instance, your base panel should be 18 x 28cm (7¼ x 11¼ inches).

Assembling the mould

1. With a ruler and pencil, mark the dimensions of the bag mould onto cardboard pieces.

2. Carefully cut out the marked panels from the cardboard using scissors or a utility knife.

3. Stand the front panel upright on a flat surface. Secure one of the side panels to the edge of the front panel using tape, forming a right angle. Repeat the process with the other side panel, attaching it to the opposite edge of the front panel.

4. Attach the back panel to the free edges of the side panels in the same way.

5. Finally, add the base panel to complete the mould and, for extra stability, wrap the entire mould with tape.

Braided headband

Whether worn across the forehead, pushed back or even paired with a chignon, headbands have been having a moment. The inspiration for this unique headband came to me when I had some braids left over from another project. I decided to weave them together and, ta-da, four individual braids seamlessly merged into one large braid. Don't hesitate to adapt this project so you can use up any surplus materials from your other makes.

Materials
Headband blank
150g (5¼oz) raffia
Measuring tape
Scissors
Weight
Pins
Large peg
Rubber bands
Long-eyed needle

1. Begin by measuring your headband from end to end and doubling that number (for instance, the one used here is 38cm/15 inches; 38cm/15 inches x 2 = 76cm/30 inches). Allowing a few extra centimetres, aim to make a braid 80cm/31½ inches long.

Braiding the raffia

2. Bundle 8 strands of raffia together and use an additional strand to tie them at the ends. Place the ends under a weight to prevent movement while braiding.

3. Divide the strands into 4 groups of 2 for a 4-strand braid, numbered 4–1 from the outer left to the outer right.

5. Once your braid starts to take shape, measure its width – we aim for a width of 1cm (⅜ inch), so add more raffia if necessary.

6. As you continue, ensure you create a flat braid by using a weight to flatten it as it lengthens.

7. Keep braiding, adding raffia as needed (see step 3, page 105), until you achieve a length of 80cm (31½ inches).

8. To finish, wrap another piece of raffia around the braid, as at the beginning (see step 2, left), and tie a double knot to prevent it from unravelling. Tidy up the braid by trimming all the ends and any excess raffia from where you added new strands.

9. As the width of the headband is 4cm (1⅝ inches), repeat steps 2–8 until you have made 4 individual braids, each measuring 80cm (31½ inches) long x 1cm (⅜ inch) wide, to cover the entire headband.

10. Now, create a master braid by wrapping a strand of raffia around the ends of your 4 individual braids and tying a knot slightly looser than when you made the individual braids (see step 2, left). Place the ends under your weight and do a 4-strand braid. Secure the end of the braid as before with a piece of raffia (see step 8, above).

Attaching the braid

11. Fold the master braid in half to locate the middle and secure it to the centre of the headband with a peg. Working on one half at a time, lay the first half of the braid flat along the headband towards one end. Fold it over the end and along the inside of the headband to the middle, securing it in place with rubber bands as you progress and repositioning the peg when you reach the middle.

12. Now it's time to stitch the first half of the master braid to the base to secure it in place. Thread your needle with a piece of raffia.

13. Working along one edge, begin stitching from one end of the headband to the middle. Guide the needle through two layers of braids. Before pulling the stitching material all the way through, tie a knot to secure it. Slant the stitches from right to left to conceal them as much as possible.

14. When you reach the middle, secure the stitching by tying a knot. Cut the excess raffia and repeat on the other side so that the other two edges are stitched together.

15. With one half of the headband secured, finish laying the rest of the master braid onto the base, ensuring the two ends meet neatly in the middle on the inside, with a small overlap.

16. Repeat steps 12–14 to stitch the edges of the other half securely to the headband.

17. Finish at the centre on the inside where the slight overlap is, guiding the needle over and under the ends of the braid to secure them, then knot and trim the stitching material, and trim off any loose ends for a neat finish.

18. Your braided raffia headband is now ready to wear. Adjust it on your head, and you're ready to go!

Clutch bag

Transition seamlessly from day to night with this half-moon clutch bag, an essential accessory for all seasons. Drawing inspiration from the moon and the colour of the night sky, I envisioned this bag as the perfect companion for those elegant evenings where you only need your phone, lipstick and keys.

Materials
100g (3½oz) black raffia
Weight
Measuring tape
Scissors
Pegs or clips
Long-eyed needle

For the lining
1 piece of leftover fabric, 28cm (11 inches) high x 51.5cm (20⅜ inches) wide
Iron and ironing board
Template (see pages 138–39)
Fabric glue or pinking shears (see step 15)
Pins
Curved needle
Sewing thread (to match the fabric or the button)
Button, 1.5cm (½ inch) in diameter

Braiding the raffia

1. Gather 15 strands of raffia and secure them together using an extra strand of raffia wound around the ends and tied in a knot. Place them under a weight to hold them still while you do the braiding.

2. Divide the bundle into 3 groups of 5 for a 3-strand braid, labelling each group bundle 1, bundle 2 and bundle 3, from left to right (see page 96).

3. Commence braiding, following steps 2–4 on pages 97–98.

4. Introduce new raffia when necessary (see step 3, page 105), until your 3-strand braid measures 10m (33 feet). Ensure consistent tension for an even braid, and keep it flat by moving the weight along its length as you work.

5. When you reach the desired length, secure the end of your braid by tying a knot with a new piece of raffia. Trim any loose ends to tidy up the braid.

Making the bag

6. Loop the end of your braid (about 1cm/ ⅜ inch) under and secure it with a peg or clip. Begin coiling the braid anti-clockwise until you form a flat circle with a diameter of 3cm (1¼ inches). Adjust the peg to hold the circle in place before stitching.

7. Thread one strand of raffia into your long-eyed needle to start stitching your bag.

8. Start stitching from the back by threading the stitching material through the central hole and tying a knot at the back to secure it. Guide the needle through two layers of braid, slanting the stitches from right to left to conceal them as much as possible.

9. Join new stitching material by knotting the piece that's running off to the new piece, and continue the stitching pattern, keeping the knots to the back.

10. Continue coiling the braid into a circle until it reaches 30cm (12 inches) in diameter. Ensure the circle looks even before completing it.

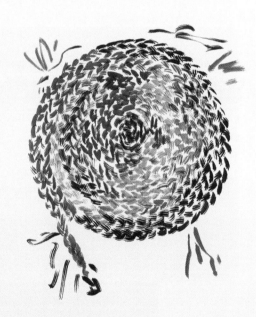

11. Finish the circle by tapering off the braid gradually and lacing the last few strands into the row below.

12. You can complete your bag at this stage by folding it in half and adding a button (see steps 17–18, opposite, for instructions).

The lining (optional)

13. Iron your lining fabric to prepare it.

14. Using the template, cut the fabric to the specified dimensions. To prevent fraying, you can apply a tiny amount of fabric glue along the raw edge and allow it to dry. Alternatively, use pinking shears, which will cut the fabric with a zigzag edge, creating a playful effect. Another option is to choose a non-woven fabric such as velvet, which naturally resists fraying.

15. Lay the raffia circle wrong side up on your workstation. Place the fabric on top, right side up, align the edges and secure it with pins.

16. Using a curved needle and matching thread, hand-sew around the edges of the circle to secure the lining fabric.

17. Fold the bag in half. Then, to create a central opening, use the same needle and thread to stitch both sides together for 10cm (4 inches), working from each corner towards the centre.

18. Finally, for extra security, sew a button centrally on the inside on one side of the opening. Use a small piece of matching thread to create a corresponding loop on the inside on the opposite side, ensuring it is the right size to accommodate your button.

Crossbody bag

As a mother, I adore a hands-free bag that combines fashion and practicality for everyday life, and this little crossbody number is just that. Perfect for urban living, travelling and those on-the-go moments, it's one of the most versatile bags and projects in this book.

Materials
100g (3½oz) raffia
Measuring tape
Scissors
Weight
Peg
Pins
Long-eyed needle

For the mould
Selection of cardboard, such as old
    parcel packaging
Ruler
Pencil
Adhesive tape
Optional: utility knife

Final bag dimensions
Width: 16cm (6⅜ inches)
Height: 16cm (6⅜ inches)
Depth: 6cm (2⅜ inches)

The mould

1. Refer to the instructions on page 109 to make a bag mould, using the following dimensions:
Front and back panels: 14 x 14cm (5½ x 5½ inches) – cut 2 panels of this size.
Base and side panels: 14 x 4cm (5½ x 1⅝ inches) – cut 3 panels of this size.

Braiding the raffia

2. Gather 20 strands of raffia and tie them together at one end using another strand of raffia. Place the ends under a weight to prevent the raffia from moving while you are braiding.

3. Divide the strands into 4 groups of 5 for a 4-strand braid, and number the groups 4–1 from left to right.

4. Commence braiding, following steps 2–4 on pages 99–100.

5. Once your braid starts to take shape, measure its width – we want a width of 2cm (¾ inch), so add raffia if needed (see step 3, page 105).

6. Continue braiding, using the weight to flatten the braid, moving it along its length as you work.

7. Add raffia as needed until your 4-strand braid is 5m (5½ yards) long.

8. To finish, wrap another piece of raffia around the braid, as at the beginning (step 2, left), and tie a double knot so the braid doesn't unravel. Tidy up the braid by cutting down all the ends.

9. Before starting the separate braid for the strap, consider how you want the bag to sit on your body. Measure yourself from one shoulder to your opposite hip, double the measurement and add an extra 2cm (¾ inch) for attaching the strap to the bag. The strap braid should be 1cm (⅜ inch) in width, so gather 12 strands and divide them into 4 groups of 3 for braiding. Repeat steps 2–8 to make a 4-strand braid to your desired length (mine is 120cm/47¼ inches).

Making the bag

10. For the base of your bag, loop one end of your braid (about 1cm/⅜ inch) underneath and secure it with a peg. As the width of the braid adds to the length of the base with each row, begin by measuring 14cm (5½ inches). Working on a flat surface, fold the braid back on itself into a U shape, ensuring it remains in position by securing it with the peg.

11. Thread a needle with raffia and stitch from the back at the rounded bottom, connecting rows 1 and 2. If you need to join new stitching material, do it at the back of your bag base.

12. For row 3, curve the braid over row 1, taking it past the loop at the end and down the other side of row 1, so that row 1 becomes the middle row, and use the peg to hold it in place. Stitch row 3 to row 1. You now have the base of your bag, ready to build the sides.

13. Pin the mould onto the wrong side of the base, ensuring that the right side of the base becomes the bottom of the bag. Begin at one end of the base and lay the braid flat against the cardboard. Pin the braid at the intersection of the current row and the previous row. Continue this process until you have completed a full row and returned to the starting point. Commence stitching along the row that you've just pinned, removing the pins as you progress.

14. Continue building the sides of the bag and maintaining the shape using the mould.

15. When you've reached the end of your braid, finish your bag at a point when the sides look level by stitching the remaining length of braid on the inside.

16. Pin one end of the strap to each side of your bag, so the end covers the top row. Try it as a crossbody bag to ensure you're happy with it, and shorten the strap if needed.

17. When you're happy with the length of the strap, stitch the ends securely to either side of the bag using a strand of raffia, reinforcing the stitching as necessary.

Sun hat

Whether protecting you from the sun or adding the final touch to a summer ensemble, a raffia hat is a wardrobe essential. When envisioning this hat, I wanted to combine the easygoingness of a bucket hat with the sophistication of a trilby or a cloche hat. It features a narrow brim and is adorned with a plush velvet ribbon for a touch of elegance.

Materials

300g (10½oz) raffia
Weight
Measuring tape
Scissors
Long-eyed needle
Pins
Round cake dummy*, 20cm (8 inches)
   in diameter x 13cm (5 inches) deep
1m (39 inches) of velvet ribbon, 3.6cm
   (14¼ inches) wide

*The round cake dummy (typically used in baking for cake decorating) serves as a hat block – made from polystyrene, it readily accepts pins, is cost-effective and acts as a mould for our sun hat.

To measure your head, wrap the measuring tape around the widest part of your head, typically above your eyebrows and ears. This measurement is then used to determine the diameter of the cake dummy you'll require for your hat. To find the diameter of a circle from the circumference, use the following formula: diameter = circumference divided by π (Pi) (π = 3.14159). If you are between sizes, take the next size up for a more comfortable fit.

Braiding the raffia

1. Select 20 strands of raffia from your bundle, wrap an additional piece of raffia tightly around them at one end, and secure the bundle under a weight to prevent movement while braiding.

2. Divide the strands into 5 groups of 4 for a 5-strand braid. Number the groups from 5–1, from left to right in the sequence 5, 4, 3, 2, 1.

3. Keep the 5 bundles separate, forming 2 groups: bundle 5 and bundle 4 together, and bundle 3, bundle 2 and bundle 1 together. Always maintain 2 groups – 1 with 2 bundles and the other with 3 bundles. Start braiding from the group with the most bundles.

4. Commence braiding, following steps 3–6 on pages 101–103, aiming for a width of 2cm (¾inch). Keep the braid tight and use a weight to flatten it, moving it along its length as you work.

5. Continue to join in new raffia when needed, staggering the joins, until you have a braid 15m (49 feet) long.

6. To finish, wrap another piece of raffia around the braid, as at the beginning (step 1, left), and tie a secure knot. Trim all the ends.

The crown

7. Thread your needle with a piece of raffia for stitching.

8. Hold the braid flat at one end and start coiling it into a circle about 3cm (1¼ inches) in diameter.

9. When stitching, work along the edge of the braid, passing the needle through one strand to another in the adjacent row.

10. When it's time to add more stitching material, unthread your needle and knot the end of your previous piece of raffia to a new piece of raffia. Thread the needle onto the new piece of raffia and continue stitching.

11. Continue coiling and stitching until you have a circle of about 20cm (8 inches) in diameter (or the size of your hat block).

12. Pin the braided and stitched circle onto the top of your hat block, right side up.

13. Begin building the sides of the hat: work down from the crown, wrapping the braid around the hat block, following its contours.

14. Add pins as you move along, and stitch each side of the braid to the edge of the previous row. Continue until you reach the end of the hat block; the hat will be approximately 13cm (5 inches) in height.

The brim

15. To form the brim, keeping the braid flat on your work surface, wrap it around the circumference of the hat and stitch it to the edge of the last vertical braid.

16. Continue until the brim reaches the desired size, about 6cm (2⅜ inches). Ensure an even brim by completing a full round.

17. Finish by carefully stitching the end of the braid under the brim, ensuring a tidy finish on the inside of the hat.

18. Optional: Tie a piece of ribbon around the base of the hat for a touch of *je ne sais quoi.*

Hat wall

Basket walls are a beloved staple in my home, so much so that I've lost count of how many we have both in our living space and my studio. It's been fascinating to watch this trend explode in the past few years, and see how they've been dubbed 'the new gallery wall'. But, when it comes to my most-loved wearables, in the same way that some fashion-forward people display a capsule collection of their favourite pieces on a rail, I love how a hat wall effortlessly creates a dynamic focal point in any room. Here are five tips to guide you if you are inspired to make one.

1. Choose a focal wall

Select a prominent space in your home – be it in the bedroom, living room or even the hallway or foyer – to serve as the blank canvas for your hat display.

2. Use hooks

Invest in sturdy hooks to ensure your hats are securely displayed. For renters, consider using damage-free options such as adhesive Command strips to hang your hats.

3. Organize by theme or colour

Arrange your hats according to themes, colours or styles. I love a seasonal hat display, for example, grouping together wool, felt and knitted hats for an autumn/winter hat wall.

4. Mix things up

Don't be afraid to mix things up – why not add a Panama hat or a straw hat to an autumn/winter display for a refreshing twist.

5. Have fun with it

Infuse your display with personality by incorporating mirrors, artworks or other homeware accessories that complement its overall aesthetic, and regularly rotate items to change things up.

Backpack

Paired with a summer dress for a picnic or with jeans and a blazer for a city look, this backpack seamlessly blends style and functionality. It is a labour of love – from dyeing the raffia to intricately braiding it and adding the final touches. But rest assured, undertaking this project is incredibly gratifying.

Materials
800g (28¼oz) raffia
Weight
Measuring tape
Scissors
Pegs
Pins
Long-eyed needle
2 leather straps, each measuring 80cm
   (31½ inches) x 2cm (¾ inch)

For the mould
Selection of cardboard, such as old
   parcel packaging
Ruler
Pencil
Adhesive tape
Optional: utility knife

For dyeing raffia
Large saucepan or pot
4–5 black tea bags, or equivalent quantity
   of loose tea
Spoon

Final backpack dimensions
Width: 33cm (13 inches)
Height: 30cm (12 inches)
Depth: 12cm (4¾ inches)

Dyeing the raffia

To achieve the delightful light brown hue of the raffia, it's essential to dye it a couple of days before starting the braiding. If you are new to natural dyeing, consider testing the method by dyeing a couple of strands in a brewed cup of black tea before tackling the entire bundle.

1. Boil 8 litres (2 gallons) of water in a large pot and add 4–5 black tea bags, or an equivalent amount of loose tea. Adjust the quantity based on your preference for the desired shade.

2. Turn off the heat and let the tea bags steep in the water for 15 minutes.

3. Using a spoon, remove the tea bags or strain the loose tea leaves to prevent them from adhering to the raffia.

4. Submerge the bundles of raffia in the tea solution. Check the colour every 5 minutes by selecting one strand and allowing it to dry outside of the pot. Leave the raffia until the desired shade has been achieved – this can take anything from 5 minutes to a few hours.

5. Drain the raffia and ideally let it air-dry for 24 hours in a well-ventilated room.

The mould

6. Refer to the instructions on page 109 to make a bag mould, using the following dimensions:
Front and back panels: 30 x 27cm (12 x 10¾ inches) – cut 2 panels of this size.
Base panel: 9 x 30cm (3½ x 12 inches) – cut 1 panel of this size
Side panels: 9 x 27cm (3½ x 10¾ inches) – cut 2 panels of this size.

Braiding the raffia

7. Bundle 28 strands of raffia, tying them together at one end with an additional strand. Place them under a weight to prevent movement during braiding.

8. Divide the strands into 4 groups of 7 for a 4-strand braid and number them 4–1 from left to right.

9. Commence braiding, following steps 2–4 on pages 99–100. Measure the braid's width as it takes shape; you are aiming for a width of 3cm (1¼ inches), so add more raffia if needed (see step 3, page 105).

10. Continue braiding, ensuring the braid is flat by using a weight to flatten it as it lengthens. Join in more raffia as necessary, making sure to stagger the joins, until you have a braid 20m (22 yards) long.

11. To finish, wrap another piece of raffia around the braid, as in step 7, above, and tie a double knot to prevent it from unravelling. Trim away all the ends and any excess raffia.

Making the bag

12. For the base of your backpack, loop one end of your braid (about 2cm/¾ inch) underneath and secure it with a peg. As the width of the braid adds to the length of the base with each row, begin by measuring 27cm (10¾ inches). Working on a flat surface, fold the braid back on itself into a U shape, ensuring it remains in position by securing it with the peg.

13. Thread your needle with a piece of raffia. Stitch rows 1 and 2 together, starting from the back at the rounded bottom of the U shape.

14. Shape row 3, curving the braid over row 1 and stitching it to it, edge to edge.

15. Continue the process to add row 4. After stitching row 4, you should have a base 12cm (4¾ inches) wide.

16. Start building the sides of your backpack. Pin the mould onto the wrong side of the base, ensuring the right side of the base becomes the bottom of the backpack. Begin at one end of the base and lay the braid flat against the mould. Pin the braid at the intersection of the current row and the previous row. Continue this process until you have completed a full row and have returned to the starting point. Commence stitching along the row that you've just pinned, removing the pins as you progress.

17. Continue wrapping and stitching the braid around the mould to build up the sides of your backpack until you've completed 7 rows.

18. We're now going to make the top of the backpack narrower than the bottom by gradually decreasing the width of the bag in rows 8, 9 and 10. Remove your backpack from the mould. Start pinning row 8, but when you reach the first side of your backpack, instead of placing the braid directly on top of the previous row for a straight side, position the braid inwards so it sits about 1cm (⅜ inch) inside the edge and pin it in place. Do the same when you reach the other side of row 8 before stitching the whole row. Repeat the process for rows 9 and 10 to continue decreasing the width of your bag.

19. When you reach the end of your braid, stitch the remaining braid on the inside.

20. Add your straps by marking points at the front and back with pins. Using the needle, thread a piece of raffia through the pre-made holes in your straps and tie a double knot on the inside to secure. Repeat for the second strap.

21. You're done! This backpack is perfect for everyday use, though it's not recommended for carrying heavy loads.

Shopper bag

This classic basket bag is my dream bag – the perfect companion for a day of shopping, going to work or a leisurely afternoon on the beach. It's spacious enough to carry all your essentials, yet not so large that things get lost in it. The intricate 5-strand braid adds an extra touch of elegance. While this project may seem more complex than some, with a bit of practice, you'll effortlessly master it and become the envy of all your friends.

Materials
800g (28¼oz) raffia
Weight
Measuring tape
Scissors
Pegs
Long-eyed needle
Pins

For the mould
A selection of cardboard, such as old
    parcel packaging
Ruler
Pencil
Adhesive tape
Optional: utility knife

Final bag dimensions
Base: 35 x 15cm (13¾ x 6 inches)
Height: 28cm (11 inches)
Width at top edge (bag widens like a reversed
    trapezoid): 50cm (19¾ inches)
Depth: 15cm (6 inches)
Straps: 4-strand braids, each measuring
    70cm (27½ inches) x 2cm (¾ inch)

The mould

1. Refer to the instructions on page 109 to make a bag mould, using the following dimensions:
Front and back panels: 32 x 47cm (12½ x 18½ inches) – cut 2 panels of this size.
Base panel: 32 x 12cm (12½ x 4¾ inches) – cut 1 panel of this size
Side panels: 47 x 12cm (18½ x 4¾ inches) – cut 2 panels of this size.

Braiding the raffia

2. Gather around 30 strands of raffia and tie them together at one end with an additional strand. Place the bundle under a weight to prevent movement during braiding.

3. Divide the strands into 5 groups of 6 for a 5-strand braid, and number them from 5–1, from left to right (sequence: 5, 4, 3, 2, 1).

4. Keep the 5 bundles separate, forming 2 groups: bundle 5 and bundle 4 together, and bundle 3, bundle 2 and bundle 1 together. Always maintain 2 groups – one with 2 bundles and the other with 3 bundles. Start braiding from the group with the most bundles, following steps 3–6 on pages 101–103.

5. Once your braid is taking shape, check for an even width (aim for 3cm/1¼ inches). Join in new raffia when necessary (see step 3, page 105), staggering the joins, until you have a braid 20m (22 yards) long.

6. To finish your braid, wrap another piece of raffia around the braid, as at the beginning (step 2, left). Tidy up the braid by cutting down all the ends that are sticking out.

7. For your bag straps, braid 2 x 4-strand braids, 2cm (¾ inch) wide and 70cm (27½ inches) long (see pages 98–100).

The base

8. For the base of your bag, loop one end of your braid (about 1cm/⅜ inch) underneath and secure it with a peg. As the width of the braid adds to the length of the base with each row, begin by measuring 26cm (10¼ inches). Working on a flat surface, fold the braid back on itself into a U shape, ensuring it remains in position by securing it with the peg.

9. Thread your needle with a piece of raffia and start stitching the adjacent edges of rows 1 and 2 together.

10. Continue to build your base until it measures approximately 15cm (6 inches) wide and comprises 5 rows.

The sides

11. Pin the mould onto the wrong side of the base, ensuring that the right side of the base becomes the bottom of the bag. Begin building the first side rows by pinning and then stitching rows on top of each other. Use a strand of raffia and a long-eyed needle to stitch the edge of each row to the adjacent edge of the previous row.

12. After row 3, start to give the bag its inverted trapezoid shape. To do this, begin by pinning and stitching the front panel of row 4. When you reach the first side of that row, position the braid so that it sits slightly outwards and not directly on top of the previous row. Measure 15cm (6 inches) for the side width, then add 1cm (⅜ inch) for a total of 16cm (6⅜ inches), and pin the braid in place. Stitch to secure. Repeat the same process as you reach the other side of row 4.

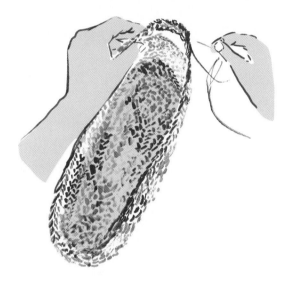

16. Pin one braided strap centrally on the front of the bag and the other on the back. Position the ends between row 2 and row 3 from the top edge and approximately 13cm (5 inches) apart. Try the bag out and make sure you are happy with the length of the straps and their position, then stitch them securely in place.

13. Continue stitching the bag upwards, gradually increasing its width after each row by following the process outlined in step 12 and remembering to add an extra 1cm (⅜ inch) on each side. As you work, pay attention to the tension and consistency of your stitching for an even shape on both sides.

14. When you've reached the end of your braid, finish your bag when it looks level by stitching the remaining braid on the inside.

15. Trim off any excess raffia strands to create a neat appearance.

Transitioning between seasons

It may be tempting to pack away your woven accessories when the temperature drops – after all, they are typically associated with the spring and summer seasons. However, with a few thoughtful choices these pieces can make a surprising yet stylish appearance in your autumn and winter wardrobes, too.

1. Mixing textures

Mix your woven accessories with heavier fabrics such as wool, suede or leather to seamlessly transition them into colder seasons. For example, pair a raffia sun hat with a chunky knit sweater and corduroy trousers, or match a raffia clutch bag with a tweed coat and ankle boots. This mix of textures creates a nice shift but also a continuation between the seasons.

2. Seasonal colours

Consider weaving your accessories in darker shades, such as deep reds, burgundies, blacks and browns or earthy tones achieved through natural dyeing (see pages 50–1). These colours naturally complement an autumn/winter wardrobe and can effortlessly become part of your everyday style.

3. Leather accents

To balance the sometimes casual and summery vibes of woven accessories, elevate them with leather accents. Think of adding leather straps to a backpack or leather handles to a basket bag for a touch of edginess and a bit more structure. This not only enhances the aesthetic but also ensures your pieces can withstand daily use and potential wear and tear.

4. Add seasonal elements

Enhance your woven accessories by incorporating seasonal elements. For instance, tie a velvet scarf around the handles of your raffia basket bag or line one of your bags with faux fur for a snug and cosy feel. These simple customizations not only elevate the autumn/winter aesthetic but also add a sense of warmth and uniqueness to your pieces.

5. Make a statement

Treat your woven accessory as a statement piece and make it the focal point of your outfit – after all, cultivating your own style means embracing individuality. Rock an all-black or neutral outfit and have your woven earrings do the talking and spark up conversations.

Template

This is a full size template so simply trace, photocopy, or scan and print to actual size, ensuring to fold the fabric in half to create the complete circle.

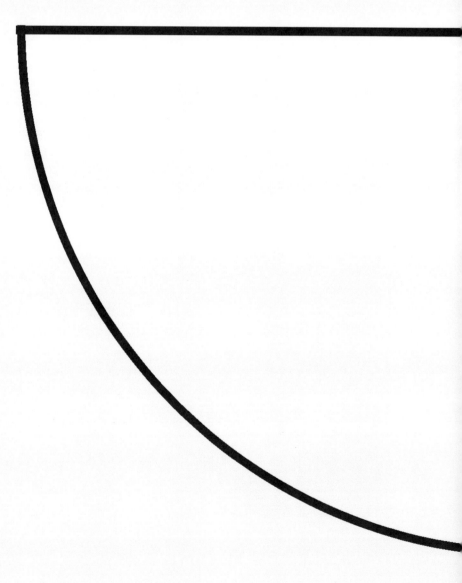

Fold

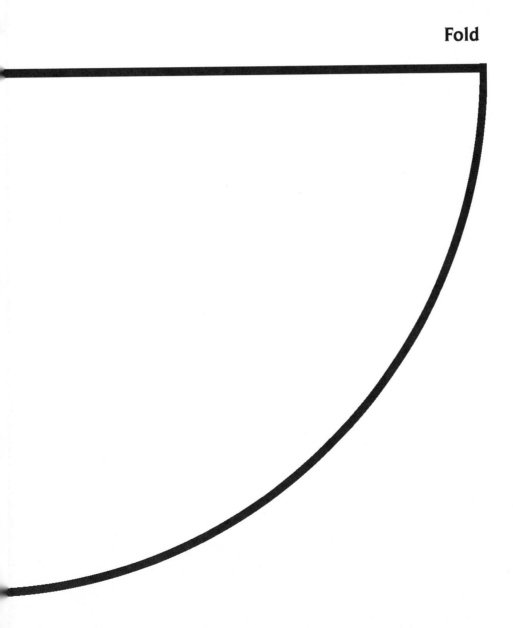

Resources

When compiling this list, I've curated a selection of reliable suppliers with whom I shop regularly. Although these items are accessible online, I encourage you, whenever possible, to opt for in-person purchases. This not only guarantees the quality and finish of the materials but also promotes the ethos of shopping small and supporting local businesses – a vital aspect of sustainable crafting.

Raffia
Nutscene
nutscene.com

Cotton Rope
MacCulloch & Wallis
macculloch-wallis.co.uk

La Basketry
labasketry.com

Centre Cane and Cane Tools
Fred Aldous
fredaldous.co.uk

Somerset Willow Growers
willowgrowers.co.uk

Basket base with pre-drilled holes
Fred Aldous
fredaldous.co.uk

Leather Handles and Straps
Leather Needle Thread
leatherneedlethread.com

Mirror
Etsy
Etsy.co.uk

Earring Hooks
The Bead Shop
the-beadshop.co.uk

Headband Base
Etsy
Etsy.co.uk

Additional Tools
Your local craft or haberdashery shop

Acknowledgements

It feels surreal to find myself at this stage once again, and I am truly grateful for the opportunity to share my passion with you all. As an avid book lover, the dream of becoming an author has always been on my mind, and to have now penned two books is nothing short of incredible.

Throughout this journey, there have been incredible individuals who have stood by me, giving me superpowers and instilling in me the confidence and vision to make this book a reality.

First and foremost, I'd like to thank my family for their unwavering support. A special mention goes to my calm, kind, and loving husband – for keeping me fed, calm, and rational when things felt overwhelming.

To my extended family – my friends – who have been constant cheerleaders since I embarked on this basket journey many moons ago, your support has never gone unnoticed.

A heartfelt thank you to Alice, Alita, Awa, Asu, Anna, Astou, Victoria, Melo, and Mäeva for their friendship and most importantly their help when I desperately needed it, whether it be driving across town to pick up some craft supplies, lending props for a shoot, or graciously offering to take Senna for a few hours when I was on a tight deadline.

To the incredible team at Quadrille, and most importantly Harriet, Ore, and Katy – thank you for making this book a reality. Who knew the best idea would come to me 6 months postpartum, sleep deprived but 100% hungry for more.

Tams, it has been an honour collaborating with you. Thank you for infusing this project with your thoughtful touches.

To Alex Mooney, you've been a constant throughout every milestone, from my first major campaign to capturing my wedding. I couldn't have imagined anyone else by my side for this book. Your talent behind the camera knows no bounds, and I am endlessly thankful you were with me to beautifully capture this new baby.

To Claire Robinson, thank you for making things happen at Toast – this mama needed to feel amazing and your clothes did just that.

To Lea Wieser, from our inaugural La Basketry & Arktaip collaboration to this. Here's to more in the future!

To Ruth Bewsey, thank you for championing both myself and La Basketry. Being a Daisy girl is a joy, and I am forever grateful for your magical creations.

And finally, to my loyal customers, the people who've joined one of my workshops, done one of my courses, or simply continue to send a word of encouragement – merci, merci, merci!

About the author

Tabara N'Diaye is a creative designer, author, and the founder of La Basketry, a vibrant lifestyle brand that originated from her passion for handwoven homeware and accessories crafted in collaboration with female artisans in her native Senegal.

Driven by a mission to redefine basket-making as 'fun and accessible', Tabara has fostered a community of basket enthusiasts through innovative projects, engaging workshops, DIY kits, and her acclaimed debut book *Baskets*, translated into five languages alongside English since its publication in 2019.

She has also made appearances on television in France and the UK, further showcasing her dedication to her craft.

It's woven into her DNA
labasketry.com

Managing Director Sarah Lavelle
Editorial Director Harriet Butt
Editor Oreolu Grillo
Copy Editor Zia Mattocks
Design and Art Direction Katy Everett
Photographer Alexandra Mooney
Illustrator Aurelia Lange
Prop Stylist Tamineh Dhondy
Head of Production Stephen Lang
Production Controller Gary Hayes

The author wishes to thank Arkitaip, Betty
Etiquette, Daisy London, Lowie, Thread The Word
and Toast for their generous loan (and support) for
the photoshoot.

Published in 2024 by Quadrille Publishing Limited

Quadrille
52–54 Southwark Street
London SE1 1UN
quadrille.com

Cataloguing in Publication Data: a catalogue record
for this book is available from the British Library.

ISBN 978 1 83783 190 6

Printed in China using soy inks